Irish History

Strange but True

Irish History

Strange but True

Colm Wallace

The History Press

First published 2026

The History Press
97 St George's Place, Cheltenham,
Gloucestershire, GL50 3QB
www.thehistorypress.co.uk

British Library Cataloguing in Publication Data.
A catalogue record for this book is available from the British Library.

ISBN 978 1 83705 135 9

Typesetting and origination by The History Press.
Printed and bound in Great Britain by TJ Books, Padstow, Cornwall.

MIX
Paper | Supporting responsible forestry
FSC® C013056
FSC www.fsc.org

The History Press proudly supports
Trees for Life
www.treesforlife.org.uk

EU Authorised Representative: Easy Access System Europe
Mustamäe tee 50, 10621 Tallinn, Estonia
gpst.request@easproject.com

About the Author

Colm Wallace is a native of Renvyle, Co. Galway. Married with four children, he works as a national school teacher and has completed a Masters in History at the University of Galway. This is his fourth book.

Contents

Introduction

All histories of Ireland are abridged, as it would not be possible to fit every significant event or turning point into one publication. *Irish History: Strange but True* does not attempt to give an exhaustive account of all periods of Irish history. It does not give a detailed account of major eras of change in Ireland, such as the Famine or the War of Independence. Rather, the aim is to pick out some of the stranger and lesser-known events within these periods and show that Ireland truly is, and always has been, a place apart with a history worth telling.

Undoubtedly, the past seems all around in Ireland, and you do not have to travel far to happen upon an ancient monument or a crumbling castle rising out of the landscape. But Ireland had a strange and storied history long before humans even set foot upon its green fields. The world is over 4 billion years old and the land that we now call Ireland was once a part of the great landmass of Pangea. By the time the world map had settled into a pattern recognisable to us today, the island lay at the western edge of Europe. The mountains of the country were already forming some 500 million years ago, but rocks aged 1.7 billion years can be found on Inishtrahull Island off Co. Donegal. When the final Ice Age thawed, the melting glaciers deposited soil and sand and the varied topography of Ireland began to take shape. The warmer climate that occurred in the aftermath allowed flowers and trees to bloom. Animal life followed, but there are fossilised tetrapod footprints on Valentia Island in Co. Kerry that are, at close to 400 million years old, among the oldest recorded instances of vertebrate life on land in the entire world, although this was when Ireland was south of the equator and the climate was very different than that which we know today. Many animals that are no longer found in the wild today, such as wolves and wild boars, were abundant in this mystical Ireland of long ago. Bears even called Ireland home and may have lived alongside the first settlers. Conversely, animals that are now a major part of the Irish landscape, such as cows and sheep, were unknown.

The first Irish people only arrived in around 8000 BC, their existence a drop in the ocean of time. Perhaps they crossed the narrow strip of water between Scotland and the northern part of the island, although the sea levels were lower at the time, potentially making this a simpler task of walking over marshy wetlands. The wet climate in Ireland was a drawback but it must have seemed a fertile hunting and fishing territory for adventurers, the rivers and lakes teeming with fish and the heavily forested countryside full of animals that could be a potential source of food. It was long believed that Mount Sandel in Co. Derry was the earliest example of human life in Ireland that has been excavated by archaeologists, although, in recent years, bones from reindeer that appear to have been killed by humans have been discovered that predate Mount Sandel and cast doubt on former certainties. Regardless, the first people probably spread across the island over time but did not live in permanent settlements, residing temporarily near the coasts and rivers where they often constructed temporary wooden huts with roofs made from rushes or animal skins to withstand the unpredictable weather. They then moved on. This nomadic lifestyle means that there are few traces of these early Irish, although this kind of life of hunting and gathering with stone tools may have lasted for 3,000 years.

Life would change slowly but surely. New materials and technologies such as bronze would come from abroad, and others would be discovered in abundance at home. New people would also come to these shores, few arriving in peace. Celts, Vikings, Normans, Planters. Each episode and each wave of immigration would change the island incrementally. Strange languages came to these shores and new rivalries between various sects exploded into life. Ireland was never truly united, and long before battles with Britain occurred, the Irish were at war with one another. But it was not all conflict. There was also music and dance, legends and storytelling, wonderful artwork from the earliest times, architecture and buildings that boggle the mind today and many other strange and wonderful occurrences that combine to tell the strange story of our ancient land.

1

Odd Tales of Old Ireland

The Earliest Irish Settlers

There are strange mysteries related to prehistoric Ireland. A prominent example is the enormous 5,000-year-old stone tomb of Newgrange in Co. Meath. The structure is 85m wide and the outer door leads into an inner chamber, via a narrow passageway complete with ornate stone carvings. Incredibly, the tomb was orientated so that the sunlight illuminates the inner chamber on just one day a year, 21 December, the Winter Solstice and the shortest day of the year. How, and indeed why, the builders went to such efforts to orientate the tomb in this way is a mystery, but as the centuries passed, the importance of the site was lost to time. Grave robbers may also have visited Newgrange and removed the valuables that had been deposited there, denying us the chance to know about what was left in the tomb and to gain an understanding of its significance.

Many archaeologists believe that Newgrange was erected as a temple and burial site. But to honour whom, in these pre-Christian times? Perhaps it was to worship the sun, explaining why it was built to align with the Winter Solstice. Like the Egyptian Pyramids, there are also questions about how it was constructed with the rudimentary technology and tools available 5,000 years ago. Even more bafflingly, many of the heavy stones needed to construct the tomb came from coastal locations, some 12 miles away, while the heavy quartz cannot be found locally and

The Entrance to Newgrange. (Photograph by the author)

is likely to have originated in the Wicklow Mountains, 50 miles distant. How could it have been transported this vast distance?

The Céide Fields are also of great interest to archaeologists. Situated in Co. Mayo, the site is considered to be the most extensive Neolithic find in Ireland and may be the oldest field system discovered in the world, although it was only properly excavated in the 1970s. The fields, complete with extensive stone walls, were buried under layers of bogs over millennia but seem to show a sophisticated farming operation. Mount Sandel Wood goes back even further and is the earliest verifiable settlement in Ireland, dating back over 9,000 years. Archaeologists discovered flint tools, suggesting that Stone Age hunters dwelt here, probably fishing in the nearby natural weir. Significant finds such as these tell us a little about our prehistoric ancestors, who must have been a resourceful lot. Other finds hint at a darker reality. Clonycavan Man, discovered by farmers cutting turf in a bog in Co. Meath in 2003, died from three blows of an axe to his head in what appears to have been a ritual killing. His body was well preserved by the peaty soil but his origins and the reasons for his killing will never be known. He was not the only ancient person to suffer a violent death, either. In August 2011, a Born na Móna worker named Jason Phelan happened upon a well-preserved body in a bog near Cashel, Co. Laois. The body was of a young high-status adult male who had been killed violently, perhaps in a human sacrifice, an event that had occurred in 2,000 BC, just after bronze had come to Ireland.

Bronze was a game-changer. The Irish had been using copper for generations, primarily in the southern part of the country, but the discovery in western Asia that combining this metal with tin at high temperatures created a stronger metal called bronze revolutionised the world. This new material enabled the production of more durable tools and weapons, making farming and land clearing much easier. Bronze Age people also made decorative pieces, as a hoard discovered near Mooghaun Hillfort in south Clare in 1854 illustrates. As three labourers were levelling the ground for the building of the railway from Ennis to Limerick, they discovered a small stone-built cist that held up to 300 fine objects. The workmen believed the objects to be ordinary items of brass, but soon realised that they were far more ancient and valuable pieces. It transpired that the hoard was from the Bronze Age and the men sold on much of the loot to goldsmiths in Limerick and Dublin, keeping the affair relatively quiet. Many of the pieces were melted down, sadly, although a small number did eventually end up in museums. The sellers made hundreds of pounds, although it is believed that what they sold was worth far more. Ireland as a nation lost more still, with most of these priceless pieces forever lost to history.

In around 600 BC, a new group known as the Celts arrived to Ireland from mainland Europe, bringing new skills and innovations that contributed to the island's development. The Celts probably came incrementally in small groups but they proved powerful – they had mastered the smelting of iron ore into iron, an even more durable metal for making tools than bronze. There is a question as to whether this technology was already being utilised by the Irish, however. The Lackan Spearhead was discovered in Co. Westmeath in the 1990s and dates from around 700 BC, throwing doubt on former historical certainties. While the Celts were not a completely peaceful people, as evidenced by their iron weapons that have been discovered, the extent of violence associated with their arrival is unclear. However, weapons predating the Celtic period have also been discovered in Ireland and, as Cashel and Clonycavan Man show us, the Irish who inhabited these shores before the Celts were not immune to violent acts themselves.

The Celts and their Beliefs

The arrival of the Celts changed the island of Ireland forever. They were storytellers and the legends they told of Ireland's past live on to this day. Celtic people believed in an ancient race, the Firbolgs. In Celtic mythology, it was believed that various members of the Firbolg tribe landed in different parts of the island long before the Celts themselves. They were said to have met at the sacred Hill of Tara, where they united their forces and divided the island into five provinces: Ulster, Munster, Connacht, Leinster, and Meath. Even the Irish language term for province, 'cúige', is derived from 'cúig', meaning 'five', although today there are only four provinces, Meath having long been subsumed into Leinster. In ancient times, each province had its own distinct laws and identity. Trefuilgnid, a mythical spirit figure from Irish folklore, described the provinces thus: learning was in Connacht to the west; there was war in Ulster to the north; wealth was the preserve of Leinster, to the east; music and art were to be found in Munster to the south; and kingship was in Meath to the centre, the home of Tara.

The Celts believed that a family of five brothers once presided over a province each. They ruled the land until the coming of the Tuatha dé Danann, the people of the Celtic goddess Danu, who arrived to Ireland, burned their boats and faced the Firbolg, demanding half of Ireland for themselves. The Firbolg refused their demand and a fierce battle lasting four days was fought between the two tribes. The Tuatha dé Danann eventually conquered the Firbolg, winning the island of Ireland for themselves at the Battle of Moytura in modern-day Co. Mayo. Danu, or Anu, was just one of many gods and goddesses worshipped by the Celts, each associated with a powerful force, for good or ill. Danu is associated with fertility, wisdom and the wind, for example. Lug, or Lugh Lámhfada, was the god of fighting, music and poetry. Lughnasa, the Irish word for August, is named in his honour. Eriú is another important Celtic deity and it is said that it was from her that Éire, or Ireland, got its name. Women were powerful and important figures in Celtic times and not to be trifled with, as the following story of the Celtic goddess Macha attests. Enraged that her husband had forced her to race against the king's horse when she was heavily pregnant, Macha laid a powerful curse on all the men of Ulster: when danger approached, all fighting men in the province would be struck down with the pain of childbirth for nine days.

Irish Legend or Irish History?

By the time of Christ's birth, Ireland was a mixture of the Celts and the original inhabitants. It had not escaped world attention either, and a famous Greek astronomer and cartographer, Ptolemy, included Ireland on his world map, which he drew up in AD 140. Considered to be the oldest surviving representation of Ireland, it was quite accurate for the time. It did not feature the mythical island of Hy-Brasil, which would be shown to the west of Ireland, deep in the Atlantic Ocean, in numerous later maps. Where did the idea of this mysterious island come from? Old Irish legends stated that there was indeed an island in this location, covered in fog and often invisible to the naked eye, except on one day every seven years when it revealed itself.

Indeed, legend and history in Ireland are often interlinked and hard to separate. Queen Medb is just one example, historians are unsure if she was a real person and a warrior queen or whether she was simply a legendary metaphor for Ireland. Medb is certainly mentioned frequently in ancient Irish annals, and she is believed by some to have been born around 50 BC, the daughter of an early High King of Ireland. The story goes that upon reaching adulthood, she married Conor Mac Nessa, the King of Ulster. However, she eventually left Conor, exercising her rights under Brehon Law, which granted women the power to own property and to choose their partners. In this system, marriage was not considered a sacrament but rather a contract that could be as short or as long as both parties desired.

Medb married several more times, including to a warrior named Ailill, and she bore nine children. Together, she and Ailill took control of Connacht, the powerful western province. The couple later quarrelled over wealth, with Ailill claiming they were equal in every way except for his prized white bull, Finnbhennach. Enraged, Medb instigated the Cattle Raid of Cooley (Táin Bó Cúailnge) by sending her army to seize the best bull in Ireland from another chieftain, Dáire Mac Fiachna, after he refused to give it up willingly. This led to a bloody conflict between Connacht and Ulster, resulting in thousands of deaths, including that of the legendary warrior Cúchulainn. Medb is said to have survived the battle and lived for several more years until her death, which came about when she was struck by a hard piece of cheese fired from a slingshot. Was she a historical figure or an Irish legend? Even her burial site is disputed, some sources suggesting she is buried at Knockma Hill, 5 miles west of Tuam, Co. Galway, while others claim she rests at Knocknarea in Co. Sligo or Rathcroghan in Co. Roscommon. Regardless of the location, it is said that her body was placed upright, facing her old enemies in Ulster.

The sources of Irish mythological stories are so ancient that, in many cases, their true origins will be forever a mystery. Those who passed down the stories originally did so orally, so that the seanchaís of the early twentieth century were often telling versions of stories from hundreds of years before. Many threads run through the old legends of Ireland: heroism, magic, mystery, revenge and love for Ireland among them. One of the most famous tales of Irish mythology is the Children of Lir, a story with a mixture of pagan and Christian influences that is learned by every Irish child at school to this day. In the tale, a wicked and jealous stepmother named Aoife casts a spell on the four children of her husband, the chieftain Lir, condemning them to 900 years as swans on three water bodies: 300 years on Lough Derravaragh in Co. Westmeath, 300 more on the freezing cold Sea of Moyle between Ireland and Scotland, and 300 final years on Inishglora, off Mayo's western coast. After the 900 years, the swans are turned back into humans, now old and frail. They then meet St Patrick, who teaches them about Christianity. This ancient story is often thought to be a parable for the history of Ireland, the four children representing the four provinces of Ireland who seemed doomed to hundreds of years of foreign oppression.

A second legendary tale that continues to captivate the Irish to this day is that of Niamh and Oisín in Tír na n-Óg, the land of eternal youth. Oisín is a strong and powerful warrior, the son of the legendary Fionn Mac Cumhaill. On a hunting expedition he encounters the beautiful Niamh of the Golden Hair, a woman who tells him she had travelled across the sea to declare her love and to bring him back to Tír na n-Óg. Perhaps this was Hy-Brasil. She promises that there is no sadness or misfortunate in her home and Oisín, captivated by Niamh and her stories, reluctantly agrees to leave his father and friends behind and go with her. The pair live happily for what seems like a few years, but Oisín longs to make a return visit to Ireland to see those dearest to him. Niamh warns him that the Ireland he left behind is no more but he persists. Reluctantly agreeing that he go, Niamh warns him not to set his foot upon Irish soil or he will never be able to return to Tír na n-Óg. When he finally reaches Ireland, Oisín discovers that hundreds of years have passed. All is changed utterly, and everyone he knew in his youth is long gone and forgotten by the native population, who seem small and weak to him and in thrall to a Church that was unknown in his youth. He later sees some men attempting to lift a boulder and, bending down from his horse, he tries to help them lift the stone but accidentally falls from the saddle, ageing hundreds of years instantly due to the passing of time.

The Giant's Causeway. (J.W. Shepp, *Shepp's Photographs of the World*, 1892)

Both stories contain magic and mystery and were of almost sacred significance to the population who heard them. Even some natural features give a nod to Irish mythological stories. The Giant's Causeway in Co. Antrim, for example, is said to be named after a local legend involving the giant Fionn Mac Cumhaill. According to the myth, Fionn built the causeway as a bridge to Scotland to challenge a rival giant named Benandonner. When Fionn saw how large Benandonner was, he changed his mind, however, and ran home before disguising himself as a baby, placing himself in a huge crib. When Benandonner arrived to Ireland, he entered Fionn's house, to be greeted by the massive infant. It was his turn to grow afraid: if that was the size of the child, how large would Fionn Mac Cumhaill himself be, he wondered? Benandonner fled from Ireland, destroying as much of the Giant's Causeway as he could on his way to deter his rival from crossing the sea to Scotland. The name of the town of Ardee in Co. Louth, meanwhile, comes from the Irish Baile Átha Fhirdhia, the town of the ford of Ferdia, Ferdia being a mythical warrior who fought Cuchulainn for four days and nights before being killed. Meanwhile, the Slieve Blooms, a low-lying mountain range in the midlands, straddling the counties of Offaly and Laois, get their name from the Irish words Sliabh Bladhma, or Bladhma's Mountain. Bladhma was a magical figure from ancient mythology who was said to inhabit the mountains to which he eventually gave his name.

Paganism Lives On

Christianity did not banish these legends, although it may have repurposed them somewhat. The Roman Empire had embraced Christianity by the close of the fourth century but the Romans themselves never invaded Ireland. They had their hands full in

England and had little use for the land they named Hibernia, 'The Land of Eternal Winter'. The religion that would come to dominate their empire, Christianity, would eventually make its way here, however, and change, or at least rearrange, many of the pagan beliefs that had dominated society before then. Paganism proved a stubborn belief system to fully eradicate, however.

Well into the twentieth century, games played at wakes were common and abhorred by the Catholic Church, who viewed them as a holdover from Pagan days. Meanwhile, a British politician named Robert Joycelyn wrote about the west of Ireland in 1841. No supporter of the Irish at the best of times, Joycelyn was particularly dismayed by what he considered to be pagan idolatry still afoot on Inishkea:

> Their state of spiritual darkness is deplorable. It is hardly to be credited that among the British islands heathen idolatry is to be found, and that a stone, carefully wrapped up in flannel, is brought out at certain periods to be adored by the inhabitants of Inishkea. When a storm arises, this heathen god is supplicated to send a wreck on their coast.[1]

The Church appears to have repurposed some Pagan festivals itself, however. St Bridget shares a name with a Celtic goddess and her feast day, marking the beginning of spring, comes at the same time as the pagan feast of Imbolc. Not all pagan festivals were immediately embraced, however. The Church was unsure about Samhain, later Hallowe'en, and what they saw as its frivolous celebration of the dead. Recognising the popularity of the feast, it eventually moved 'All Saints' Day' from May to 1 November to coincide with Samhain in an effort to Christianise the festival.

---

1 Joycelyn, R,. *Progress of the Reformation in Ireland* (1851), pp.28–9.

2

Strange Visitors Arrive to Ireland

Then in came the faraway stranger,
And scattered all over our land.
The horse and the cow, the goat and the sow,
Fell into the stranger's hand.

'To Welcome Paddy Home', Boys of the Lough

Ireland's Saints and Scholars

Christianity came to Ireland in the fifth century but, remarkably, the Irish patron saint Patrick may not have been the first to bring word of the good news. Many believe that it was in fact brought by Palladius, a bishop from Gaul, the territory now called France. However, St Patrick is credited with converting much of the country although not an Irishman at all, despite his special place in Irish hearts. He was kidnapped from his home, possibly in Wales, and was afterwards forced into slavery, spending several years tending sheep in Co. Antrim. After escaping, he trained to become a bishop and returned to Ireland in 432 to spread Christianity. Legend says he used the three leaves of the shamrock, abundant in Ireland, to explain the concept of the Holy Trinity – Father, Son and Holy Spirit – to the pagan Irish. He managed to convert many influential chiefs, who then encouraged their people to adopt the new faith.

The colour green, which we now strongly associate with St Patrick, was not the colour in which he was originally depicted. This was St Patrick's Blue, although things changed around the 1798 Rebellion when green became inextricably linked with Ireland and consequently with our patron saint. St Patrick's sister, St Darerca, is less well known but also came to Ireland and converted many people. She is believed to have given birth to seventeen sons, all of whom became bishops!

St Patrick. (Mary Frances Cusack, *An Illustrated History of Ireland*, 1868)

Another remarkable saint was St Brendan. He amassed many achievements in the sixth century, including the founding of monasteries such as Clonfert in Co. Galway. But was he the first European to reach America? Accounts indicate that St Brendan embarked on numerous sea voyages around Ireland, Wales and western Scotland before undertaking his journey to the New World. A Latin account details this journey, describing how Brendan and his fellow monks witnessed a volcanic eruption, saw crystals floating in the sea, and were pursued by a sea monster. Some sceptics questioned whether a boat made from wood and ox hides could have endured such a long journey. However, in the 1970s, a sailor and geographer named Tim Severin successfully recreated St Brendan's supposed sixth-century voyage over thirteen months and gave fresh confidence to those who believed that this Irish saint of renown may have reached America nearly 1,000 years before Christopher Columbus.

The arrival of Christianity marked the beginning of a golden era for Irish education, and the island soon became renowned as the Land of Saints and Scholars, at a time when Europe was living through the Dark Ages. Monasteries were established throughout the country, typically in secluded locations where monks could live and pray peacefully, and many well-preserved examples from this period can still be found in Ireland, at Clonmacnoise, Ardmore and Kilmacduagh, among others.

The monasteries were expertly constructed with stone and often featured guest houses, scriptoria, round towers and other remarkable buildings. Dozens of round towers still stand, up to 35m high in some cases. These may have been built to protect the monks from raiders, but the monasteries were largely serene places where young monks received their education in reading and writing. Beautiful religious manuscripts were created on

Round Towers at Clonmacnoise (left) and Glendalough. (T.O. Russell, *Beauties and Antiquities of Ireland*, 1897)

vellum by the monks, with the Book of Kells being the most famous example, today attracting up to a million visitors yearly. Interestingly, sixty pages of this beautiful work are missing, believed to have been stolen over 1,000 years ago.

Irish monks also went abroad spreading the good news. St Gall got as far as Switzerland, where he set up a hermitage in AD 612 on the site of the present-day city of St Gallen, named in his honour. Leinster native St Columbanus founded Bobbio Abbey in Italy in the early seventh century while also establishing Luxeuil Abbey in present-day France. Colmcille is among the best known of the adventurous missionaries. After founding many Irish monasteries, he travelled to the island of Iona in Scotland. He then converted many of the Pictish people of Scotland, apparently impressing them when he bade the Loch Ness Monster to stop attacking a man who was swimming in the lake.

Ireland also had many female saints who left their mark. Most famous among them is St Brigid, the founder of a monastery in Kildare, who has many miracles attributed to her. These include the tale of Brigid boldly approaching the King of Leinster and asking him for land in Kildare upon which to build a monastery. Not renowned for his generosity, the king refused. Undeterred, she pointed to her cloak and asked if she could at least have the land that it would cover. The king laughed and agreed to her bizarre request. She set her cloak down and he watched in amazement as it grew and grew, spreading across several acres. The monastery was built on the land as promised and the king, impressed by the miracle, duly converted to Christianity. St Ita was another saint with miracles attributed to her. Born of a royal family, Ita eschewed her life of privilege and lived as a nun in Killeedy, Co. Limerick, where she founded a monastery and set up schools for boys, counting St Brendan among her pupils. One miracle that is attributed to her was the taking of the head of a beheaded man and reuniting it with his body.

St Kevin was also born of a royal family but chose to embrace solitude. His new-found devotion to God caused him to forgo his possessions and commit to a simple life in a forest in the shadows of the Wicklow Mountains at Glendalough: Gleann dá Locha, the valley of the two lakes. Many monks came to live with the hermit and stories are told of wonders that occurred there, including a time when St Kevin was praying with arms outstretched and a blackbird landed on his hand and laid an egg. It was said that, due to his deep love of nature, Kevin remained in this exact position until the egg was hatched. The monastery in Glendalough's isolation is dwarfed by that of the Skellig Islands, almost 8 miles off Co. Kerry, which were also home to an early Christian monastery. It is well preserved and is today a UNESCO World Heritage Site.

The well-known St Valentine, the patron saint of lovers, was not Irish but his remains lie in this country. Born in Rome, St Valentine converted many important people within the

Beehive Huts on the Skelligs. (Photograph by the author)

Roman Empire but was beheaded by the Emperor Claudius II for his proselytising. In 1835, an Irish Carmelite priest named John Spratt visited the Eternal City. Highly regarded as a preacher, the elite of Rome eagerly gathered to hear him, and as a token of his esteem, Pope Gregory XVI gifted him the remains of Saint Valentine. They are now on display in Whitefriar Street Church in Dublin.

The importance of religion can be illustrated by the fact that many of Ireland's towns and villages are named after saints, including almost anywhere that starts with 'Kil', which usually comes from the Irish word Cill, meaning 'church'. Killarney, Kildare and Kilkenny are prominent examples, the latter coming from the Irish Cill Chainnigh, meaning 'church of Canice'. Place names in Ireland that contain the words Teampall (temple), Donagh (church) or Monaster (abbey) are common and also usually dedicated to a saint or holy place. Even the devil gets a look in. Local legend has it that Devil's Bit Mountain in Co. Tipperary got its name because the devil took a bite out of it. A small gap between a rocky outcrop and a nearby plateau is said to be the result of this bite. The story goes that the devil broke his teeth in the process and spat out the Rock of Cashel, which landed where it now stands. Additionally, in Connemara, there is a mountain called Devil's Mother, which comes from the Irish Magairlí an Deamhain (meaning 'the demon's testicles'). The origin of this peculiar name, however, remains a mystery.

The Coming of the Vikings

Also known as the Norsemen, the Vikings originated in Scandinavia and were skilled farmers in search of fertile land. Due to the scarcity of good farmland at home, combined with the harsh climate and long, dark winters, they were driven to venture overseas. The Vikings first raided Ireland in around 795, attacking Lambay Island off the coast of Co. Dublin. There, they pillaged a monastery, stealing its treasures and killing many of the monks. They had started as they meant to go on and coastal regions knew intermittent raids for the next century. Viking longships appearing on the horizon was a cause of terror. Eventually, the Norsemen grew bolder and even began to make forays up major rivers, attacking monasteries such as Clonmacnoise on the shores of the River Shannon but many miles from the coast. Violence was a regular occurrence – a massacre of horrific proportions was thought to have occurred at Dunmore Cave in Kilkenny in AD 928, when hundreds of men, women and children were killed by Vikings. Thousands of bones were discovered there in 1869, indicating that something truly terrible had occurred, although in recent years a theory has emerged that the victims had indeed been hiding in the cave from Vikings but had suffocated to death rather than been massacred.

This real fear of the marauding Vikings caused the Irish to hide their valuables wherever they could. The beautiful Ardagh Chalice, dating from around AD 750, is one of the finest examples of Irish metalwork. It was buried in a field at Reerasta, near the village of Ardagh, Co. Limerick, possibly in anticipation of a Viking raid. So good was this hiding place that it was not rediscovered until 1868, when two boys digging potatoes stumbled upon it. The equally impressive Derrynaflan Chalice was found in similar circumstances in 1980 in Co. Tipperary. Today, these are counted as two of Ireland's most prized artefacts. What other treasures could lurk beneath the Irish soil, waiting to be discovered?

The Vikings travelled further afield than Ireland, and the strong links between Ireland and Iceland are a result of their marauding. There is a remarkable amount of DNA shared by the populations of both countries. In fact, some studies suggest that over 60 per cent of Icelandic women have Irish ancestry.

The exact reason for this is difficult to know at this remove. Irish monks certainly travelled to Iceland early in the ninth century, before the Vikings ever came to its shores, and Irish may have been the first language spoken on the island. The Vikings finally descended on Iceland in AD 874, nearly a century after they first came to Ireland. Whether all the hermetic Irish monks left their new homeland at this point, and whether this was by choice or by force, is difficult to tell. Either way, many Irish women found themselves in Iceland over the coming centuries. Were they brought forcibly or did they assent to travel to the island to the north? What is clear is that Iceland had an Irish connection from its earliest settlement. Ireland is synonymous with red hair and it does have among the highest percentage of red-haired people in the world, with the Celtic nations of Scotland and Wales close behind. Unsurprisingly, Iceland also has a high percentage. It also has a town called Patreksfjörður, probably named by the first settlers in honour of St Patrick. Interestingly, it is also said that this fjord was where the first potatoes were grown in Iceland.

The Death of Brian Boru at Clontarf.
(Eleanor Hull, *The Northmen in Britain*, 1913)

Meanwhile, back in Ireland, the Vikings eventually began to settle among the native population. They proved adept urban planners and Ireland, which had no major urban settlements before their arrival, can thank them for towns and cities such as Wexford, Waterford, Dublin, Limerick and Cork, all situated on important waterways for local and international trade. They built houses with walls of post-and-wattle, using cow dung or mud as a rudimentary form of cement. Clashes with the native Irish were common, culminating in the Battle of Clontarf on Good Friday, 1014. Munster, led by Brian Boru, had grown increasingly powerful in the tenth century and, by the early eleventh century, Brian was eyeing up the entire island. By 1014, the Vikings had grown weary of his expansionism and, along with some of their Irish allies, faced him at Clontarf. It was violent in the extreme, with thousands of deaths, including that of Brian Boru, who was said to have been killed by a Viking named Brodir. The precise details of the Battle of Clontarf are shrouded in mystery. Even its exact location is unknown. Nevertheless, it was used by many patriots in the 1,000 years that followed as a glorious example of Ireland uniting to defeat a common foe, although this may not be strictly what occurred with Vikings and Irish appearing on both sides in the battle.

The Coming of the Normans

The year 1169 is often considered the beginning of British dominance over Ireland, something that would continue until 1921. Strangely, in 1169 at least, they were invited, although they would soon become a guest that would refuse to leave. The invitation came from the King of Leinster, Diarmuid Mac Murrough. Mac Murrough had lost the battle against the combined forces of Connacht and Breifne (the north-midlands region) earlier in the decade and consequently risked losing his kingdom. There had been a long-standing rivalry between Mac Murrough and the Breifne O'Rourkes, not helped by Tigernán O'Rourke's wife Derbforgaill deserting him, either by being abducted or leaving of her own accord. Either way, she ended up in Wexford in Mac Murrough's house and came to be known as Ireland's Helen of Troy. The bloody battle that followed saw Mac Murrough's forces being routed.

Rather than accept his loss, Diarmuid went to the court of King Henry II of England, begging for his help to regain his lost lands. The king could see benefits in such a venture and gave his assent for Mac Murrough to enlist the aid of some Norman lords from south Wales. Strongbow, or Richard de Clare, agreed to lead the expedition on condition that he could also take the hand of Diarmuid Mac Murrough's daughter, Aoife, as his wife, and that he would secure Leinster as his own after Mac Murrough's death. After securing agreement, Strongbow assembled a party of Normans who landed in Co. Wexford in 1169. Their army marched on Ireland and, with their sophisticated weaponry and tactics, took much of the country in a short time.

Their siege of Waterford was particularly bloody:

> Again and again, the assailants were hurled from the walls; but at length the Norman sieging skill prevailed; a breach was effected; the enemy poured into the town, and a scene of butchery shocking to contemplate ensued. Diarmuid arrived just in time to congratulate Strongbow on this important victory. He had brought his daughter Eva with him, and amid the smoking and blood-stained ruins of the city the nuptials of the Norman knight and the Irish princess were celebrated.[2]

2 Sullivan, A.M., *The Story of Ireland* (1883), p.115.

This marriage of Strongbow and Aoife went ahead in 1170. A nineteenth-century painting by Daniel Maclise depicting this wedding ceremony hangs in the National Gallery of Ireland to this day. The painting symbolises the catastrophic effects of the Norman invasion. Strongbow's foot rests upon a fallen Celtic cross, while Diarmuid Mac Murrough looks on with a pained expression. Aoife, the bride, appears crestfallen and beside her is an elderly musician slumped on that most Irish of instruments, a broken-stringed harp.

Mac Murrough did not get much time to enjoy retaking his kingdom, dying in 1171. His actions would ensure that his name lived on in Irish infamy, however.

More Irish than the Irish Themselves

The Normans, like the Vikings before them, eventually embraced their new home. Although they remained the elite of the country for centuries, over the years they picked up the Irish language, wore Irish dress and even began to play the game of hurling. The English viewed these changes with horror and the fourteenth-century Statutes of Kilkenny demanded that Normans maintain English customs. After all, Irish traditions were viewed with derision. Gerald of Wales, or Giraldus Cambrensis, epitomises the attitude towards the Irish among his countrymen. A priest and son of a Norman lord, Gerald lived in Ireland for a time and wrote his 1188 book *Topographia Hibernica* on the country. It mentioned strange wonders such as human corpses that do not rot, a stone in Munster that produced wine and a cross in Dublin that could speak. He spoke scathingly of the island's people, however, stating that 'They live on beasts only and live like beasts.' He goes on to describe a barbaric ritual in Donegal of which he had been informed:

> When the whole people of that land have been gathered, a white mare is brought forward into the middle of the assembly. He who is to be inaugurated, not as chief, but as a beast, embraces the animal before all, professing himself to be a beast also. The mare is then killed immediately, cut up in pieces, and boiled in water. A bath is prepared for the man afterwards in the same water. He sits in the bath surrounded by all his people, and all, he and they, eat of the meat of the mare which is brought to them. He quaffs and drinks of the broth in which he is bathed, not in any cup, or using his hand, but just dipping his mouth into it round about him.[3]

This is just one of the many stories of Gerald's that must have filled the people of his home country with horror. He was not the first to make outrageous claims about the Irish people. The Ancient Greek geographer Strabo, who lived around the time of Christ, stated that the people of Ierne considered it honourable to eat their dead fathers, although he also said that Ireland was situated to the north of Scotland, so perhaps he was not a reliable source.

---

3 Cambrensis, G., *The History and Topography of Ireland* (1982), pp.93–4.

3

Haunted Ireland

Strange Ancient Creatures of Ireland

There are many strange tales of haunted Ireland that have chilled the bones of natives and visitors alike over the millennia. Many have their origin in Celtic times. The Celts appear to have enjoyed a scary story and the now worldwide celebration of Hallowe'en owes its origins to the Celtic festival of Samhain, a time to mark the beginning of winter, when Celts believed the gap between the world of the living and that of the dead was at its narrowest and where the deceased walked among us in various guises. One Irish death messenger that originates from Celtic times is the cóiste bodhar, or silent coach. Even the name brought terror, evoking the image of a large black coach carrying a coffin and driven by a headless driver known as a Dullachán. The coach was said to travel the roads at night, the driver calling out the names of those doomed to die while carrying his head under his arm. Where this frightening tradition originates is uncertain but some say it is an image of the Celtic god of fertility, Crom Dubh, who

was worshiped in pre-Christian times by an ancient king of Ireland, Tigernmas. The king sacrificed humans to him annually by decapitating them.

Although the advent of Christianity should theoretically have brought an end to the worship of Crom Dubh and other Celtic gods, their spirit lived on in many cases. In the case of the headless Dullachán, terrifyingly so, and the sight of the coach was dreaded as a harbinger of death. It was whispered that once the coach came to Earth, it would not return empty.

W.B. Yeats recorded much folklore about the Dullachán, recounting how it:

> ... rumbles to your door, and if you open it, a basin of blood is thrown in your face. It is an omen of death to the houses where it pauses. Such a coach not very long ago went through Sligo in the grey of the morning, as was told me by a sailor who believed he saw it. In one village I know its rumbling is said to be heard many times in the year.[4]

Even more famous than the Dullachán may be the dreaded banshee (Bean Sí or fairy woman). It is said that the banshee's wailing shriek can be heard on a dark night when the death of a family member is close at hand, although the spirit only targeted certain families. In 1890, D.R. McAnally wrote of a lady of a prominent family who was taken ill at the family mansion:

> No uneasiness was felt on her account, as her ailment seemed nothing more than a slight cold. After she had remained indoors for a day or two, several of her acquaintances came to her room to enliven her imprisonment, and while the little party were merrily chatting, strange sounds were heard, and all trembled and turned pale as they recognised the singing

4 Yeats, W.B., *Irish Fairy Tales* (1890), p.230.

of a chorus of Banshees. The lady's ailment developed into pleurisy, and she died in a few days, the chorus being again heard in a sweet, plaintive requiem as the spirit was leaving her body.[5]

The Abhartach is yet another terrifying spectre from Irish folklore. A vampire-like dwarf creature, the Abhartach may have inspired Bram Stroker's terrifying novel *Dracula*. The Dearg Due is another of Ireland's mythical creatures with traits akin to a vampire. Her name comes from the Irish words meaning 'red bloodsucker' and she was said to seduce men and then drain them of their blood when they were relaxed in her company. With each experience, she becomes hungrier for blood.

Witches and Witchcraft

The belief that witches and witchcraft were a threat to the community was not confined to Salem, Massachusetts. In fact, there were several prominent witch trials in Ireland before the nineteenth century. These usually involved women being accused of crimes, such as demonic possession, which were almost impossible to disprove. Alice Kyteler was one woman who came under suspicion in what became known as the Kilkenny Witch Trials. Born to a wealthy Anglo-Norman family in 1263, Alice's first husband, William Outlawe, died early in their marriage. The second man she married, a prominent banker named Adam le Blund, suffered a similar fate. Both men had been wealthy and Alice was left in good financial circumstances. Her third and fourth husbands also died mysteriously, however, and whispers began to spread that all was not right with Alice. This may have

5 McAnally, D.R., *Irish Wonders* (1888), p.113.

been due to jealousy against Alice on account of her wealth and the moneylending activities she engaged in, but some posited that she had bewitched these four men and caused their deaths. Charges were laid against Kyteler and she was brought before a council who heard accusations that she was the head of a coven and had been having sexual relations with a demon. It was also heard that she had offered a sacrifice to an evil spirit consisting of nine red cocks and nine peacocks' eyes.

A local cleric, Bishop De Lederede, excommunicated Kyteler from the Church, accusing her of rejecting Christ and demanding that she be arrested and tried in front of him. She wisely refused to appear in any court led by the bishop and fled to England. When she returned a year later, however, she was arrested and charged with witchcraft. She, and several of her supposed disciples, were found guilty and sentenced to death. After being whipped through the streets of Kilkenny, Alice languished in the dungeons of Kilkenny Castle awaiting her punishment, before Roger, the brother of her first husband William, organised her escape. She again fled the country and did not return. Alice was more fortunate than her friends and associates. Her teenage maid, Petronella de Meath, was tortured and confessed to being a witch. She was burned at the stake in front of a large crowd on 3 November 1324. What became of Alice Kyteler is not known. Her son, William, was punished for his alleged role in the saga by being forced to pay for the construction of a tower on St Canice's Cathedral in Kilkenny. Eight years after the witch trial, the tower and part of the roof came crashing down inexplicably, leaving many to wonder whether it was a punishment from above for the excesses of the witch trials.

This was not the only witch trial in Irish history, although it is certainly the most infamous. The last official witch trial held on Irish soil took place in Islandmagee, Co. Antrim, in 1711. It began after an elderly woman named Ann Haltridge died following months of seizures and fits. Her niece, Mary Dunbar, moved into her home shortly afterwards and she, too, began experiencing unexplained convulsions. Dunbar claimed to have had dreams and visions in which eight local women tormented her. These women were later brought to trial. Although Mary Dunbar had died by the time of the proceedings, the women were charged, not only with witchcraft, but also with behaviours considered sinful in their strictly Presbyterian community. These included drinking alcohol, smoking, blasphemy and neglecting church attendance. All were convicted and sentenced to the pillory four times and to serve one year in prison. A man named William Sellor was also convicted for allegedly bewitching Dunbar and was sentenced to death, although no definitive records confirm whether the execution took place.

The trial of Darkey Kelly that occurred in around 1761 was also long believed to have been a witch trial, and for many generations her name became synonymous with the dark arts. The truth is even more horrific. Kelly, a brothel-keeper, was charged with the murder of five men whose bodies were discovered in the brothel she ran in Dublin. Whether she was a serial killer is hard to know at this juncture but her punishment was grotesque. She was half-hanged, before being burned alive in front of a baying crowd on Baggot Street in the capital.

As the eighteenth century progressed, official witch trials faded away, and the Irish Witchcraft Act was repealed in 1821, bringing an end to the persecution of so-called witches in Ireland. Such tales of witches in Irish folklore remained commonly told well into the twentieth century, however. Lady Jane Wilde was one of the foremost collectors of strange superstitions and ghostly tales of Ireland and she recorded numerous tales of witches. Even the *Schools' Folklore Collection* of 1937 has hundreds of stories of witches that the children collected from elderly relatives. These included widely held superstitions that witches could turn into hares, cats and other animals. The collection was a mammoth effort to gather the folklore and superstitions of Ireland, the belief being that the telling of such stories was on the wane. It was a great success and it is notable that a huge number of the stories recorded contain a supernatural theme.

More Supernatural Creatures

There was traditionally a strong belief in sea monsters in the waterways in and around Ireland also. The Oilliphéist (great worm) appeared regularly in folklore and was said to have resembled a huge water snake that could cause flooding and natural disasters. A large water snake named Caoránach was said to have had an encounter with St Patrick, who condemned it to the bottom of Lough Derg, Co. Donegal. The later nineteenth century saw an increasing number of alleged sightings of sea monsters, including at Kilkee, Co. Clare, in 1871, when several locals vowed that they had seen a terrible creature sunning itself at the water's edge. In later years, other sea monsters have reportedly been resident in Ireland, including at Lough Fadda and Lough Auna in Galway. Ireland may even have an answer to the Loch Ness Monster, found in Lough Ree, lying between Westmeath and Roscommon. In May 1960, newspapers reported the experience of three priests who had embarked on a day's fishing. At some point, one of them noticed a creature about 100 yards away that resembled a sea serpent. They later recounted that it had been some 6ft in length. Further sightings of this monster were recorded by others in the area but no conclusive evidence proving its existence has come to light.

Another interesting maritime creature is the mermaid, who regularly appears in ancient Irish tales. A merman was apparently spotted by two fishermen off the coast of Connemara in 1938. The witnesses swore that the merman could speak Irish and

The Mermaid. (Joseph Jacobs, *Celtic Folk and Fairy Tales*, 1892)

behaved aggressively towards them. The story gained legs and featured in dozens of contemporary newspapers, including the *Times of London*.

Belief in the fairies was also widely held until relatively recently. Lady Jane Wilde collected the following story in the 1880s from an elderly storyteller:

> There are many strange superstitions in the western islands. At night the dead can be heard laughing with the fairies and spinning the flax. One girl declared that she distinctly heard her dead mother's voice singing a mournful Irish air away down in the heart of the hill. But after a year and a day the voices cease, and the dead are gone for ever.[6]

6 Wilde, J. *Ancient Legends, Mystic Charms & Superstitions of Ireland* (1888), p.172.

This belief in fairies and changelings would have horrifying consequences in the case of Bridget Cleary. Bridget was a talented seamstress who lived near Fethard in Co. Tipperary in the last decade of the nineteenth century. She was an independent woman who sold eggs, was highly literate and wore gold jewellery and feathered hats, unusual for the time. Her husband, Michael, was a cooper, nine years her senior. The only apparent difference between their marriage and the marriages of others in their village was that theirs was childless. In March 1895, Bridget was bedbound, having come down with an illness, possibly bronchitis. Her husband called in a local fairy doctor, who decreed that Bridget was possessed by an evil spirit of some kind. She was force-fed herbal remedies while Michael continuously demanded to know: 'Are you Bridget Boland, wife of Michael Cleary, in the name of God?' This treatment continued for days, often with others present, including members of Bridget's family. No one intervened. On 15 March, after she refused to eat a piece of brown bread, Michael doused his wife in lamp oil and set her alight. She burned to death. He then buried her body, with the help of neighbours, before reporting her missing, telling authorities she had gone away with the fairies.

Bridget's body was quickly found in the shallow grave and Michael Cleary was charged with murder. He insisted that it had not been his wife that he had killed but a changeling. Some neighbours even backed up his ludicrous claims, one stating that he could tell that it had not been Bridget Cleary who had died because she had one leg longer than the other. Unbelievably, Michael was convicted on the lesser charge of manslaughter and sentenced to twenty years' imprisonment, serving just fifteen. Bridget's father was also dispatched to jail. Bridget, meanwhile, was buried in a pauper's grave, her family unwilling to take charge of the funeral.

Belief in fairies had begun to wane by the 1930s, as this account from Co. Cavan indicates:

Fairies were more common long ago than they are now. There was a woman whose name was Mrs McManus. One evening when she was going to milk, she saw a little fairy cobbling shoes. She went up to him and caught him. When she had a good hold of him, he said 'Look at the child behind you.' She thought it was one of her own children and she looked behind her. There was no child there at all. When she looked back the fairy was gone. There were a lot of fairies about here long ago.[7]

Ghosts of Ireland Today?

Hans Holzer's 1967 *Lively Ghosts of Ireland* told of the most famous hauntings that were still believed in Ireland at that time, and the Austrian parapsychologist visited numerous places said to be home to ghosts. He wrote that he picked up on several instances of ghostly activity and interviewed people who said they had experienced paranormal events in places as varied as Skryne Castle, Co. Meath, Maynooth College in Co. Kildare and the Olympia Theatre in Dublin, among others. In the latter venue, one workman told him that he had been lifted off his seat at one point, while others talked of mysterious glowing lights, incessant footsteps and unexplained knocking on doors. In Maynooth College, a seminary for priests, he learned of a bedroom that had been closed up in 1860 after each occupant that stayed there recounted terrifying experiences.

It is sometimes said that the coming of electricity to rural Ireland brought an end to such widespread belief in supernatural creatures. No longer were creeping shadows in the

7 'Fairies', Tomena NS, The Schools' Collection, Vol. 0963, National Folklore Collection UCD, p.543, www.duchas.ie/en/cbes/5044787/5038146

semi-darkness to be feared, with the electric light bulb hanging from the ceiling illuminating formerly dark corners of the house. Undoubtedly, there are fewer ghost stories told in modern Ireland than in the past. And yet, there are places where spirits are still widely believed to roam. Loftus Hall, a stately manor built in the fourteenth century in Co. Wexford, is possibly the most famous among them. Once styling itself as the most haunted house in Ireland, Loftus Hall was said to have been visited by a mysterious man on a dark and stormy night in 1775. Let in out of the elements by the benevolent householders, the man was invited to participate in a game of cards with the family. When a card dropped to the floor, Lady Anne Tottenham, a daughter of the house, bent to pick it up, noticing as she did so that their visitor had cloven feet. Her shriek alerted the man to her discovery and he shot up through the roof, never to be seen again. The family believed they had been in the presence of Satan himself and Anne, driven mad by the encounter, was said to have wandered the halls of the house for the rest of her life and even after her death.

Malahide Castle in Co. Dublin has also been rumoured to be home to strange occurrences. There is said to be a disappearing statue on the grounds, while the house was believed by some to be haunted by a number of ghosts, including a butler named Puck. Various tales abound of Puck's identity. He may have been a fifteenth-century butler in the castle who hanged himself, or even a jester who fell in love with a noblewoman, leading to his execution. Either way, it was said that before his death, he vowed to haunt the castle forever, and that his spirit can be found lurking in doorways waiting to play tricks on unsuspecting visitors. It is even claimed that his murky outline has appeared in photographs! Meanwhile, Duckett's Grove, a large stately home in Co. Carlow that burned down mysteriously in 1933, is said to be home to a ghostly fox hunt that can be seen traversing the local countryside before disappearing into thin air. Several witnesses have also reported hearing a mournful organ being played in the deserted ruin.

The Trinity Street Ghost is probably Belfast's most repeated ghost story. The haunting began in 1931 after a family moved into a house on the street near the city centre. They quickly sublet rooms, causing the lodgings to be overcrowded. Soon, residents began to notice doors and windows being slammed inexplicably and eerie moans coming from the coal shed. Witnesses claimed to see a glowing young man or a dark figure in a cape and hat, often on the stairs or in bedrooms. Others swore they saw a headless man or a banshee. Furniture and ornaments were thrown by unseen hands and some tenants, frightened, tied their doors shut, only to find them open by morning. Crowds began to gather nightly outside the house, hoping for a glimpse of the supernatural creature. A medium

was called in, and several newspapers sent reporters. One theory to explain the haunting suggested a man named Edward had been murdered and buried beneath the coal shed, but the landlord refused to allow digging to take place. In January 1932, the last tenants left. After that, the disturbances ceased, and no later occupants reported anything unusual, although the strange tale of the Trinity Street Ghost is told to this day.

St Michan's Church in Dublin City is another place not for the faint-hearted. The crypt in the church remains open and mummified bodies can be viewed by anyone who wishes to. These bodies are exceptionally well preserved due to the thick limestone walls and the marshy ground below them. It has some well-known people buried there, including the Sheares Brothers, hanged, drawn and quartered for their part in the 1798 Rebellion.

Other corpses' names have been lost to the mists of time, but the visible mummies include a nun who has been dead for 400 years and a man who is missing a hand and both feet, something that may have been a punishment for thievery. The macabre crypts may even have been an inspiration for Bram Stoker, the author of *Dracula*, whose family had a burial plot in the graveyard. A placard near the crypt reads: 'What you are now we used to be; what we are now, you will be ...'

4

Rebellion After Bloody Rebellion

Massacres of (and by) the Irish

One does need to consult the supernatural to read of Irish horrors. Massacres of, and occasionally by, the Irish occurred with grim regularity. A cursory glance at Irish history from the arrival of the Normans in 1169 to the War of Independence in 1921 may indicate that little occurred on the island other than rebellion after rebellion, and that the Irish were rarely blessed with good fortune in any of these encounters against a more powerful foe. There are so many uprisings, in fact, that it is difficult to recount them all. One of the earliest revolts against English rule was Silken Thomas' Rebellion. The Fitzgeralds of Kildare were of Norman descent and had long been counted among Ireland's elite. By 1534, they had lost favour with King Henry VIII, however, despite the fact that the family were related by marriage to English royalty. When Gearóid Óg Fitzgerald was imprisoned in the Tower of London, his son, Silken Thomas, heard that his father had been killed. This rumour was probably spread by the Fitzgeralds' enemies, but Silken Thomas chose to believe it and publicly announced that he no longer offered obedience to the Crown. In a show of defiance, he and his band attacked Dublin, Trim and other important settlements.

After gathering an army, the English laid siege to the Fitzgeralds' headquarters at Maynooth Castle and it was quickly destroyed by cannon fire. Thomas seems to have been offered mercy in return for surrendering at this point, causing him to believe that his life would be spared. Legend has it that shortly before his surrender, Silken Thomas played a lute under the boughs of what is now the oldest planted tree in Ireland. His optimism and trust were misplaced and no mercy was forthcoming. After two years as a prisoner in the Tower of London, Silken Thomas, alongside five of his uncles, was hanged, drawn and quartered at Tyburn.

Such violent attempts to put down uprisings presumably had the intention of deterring future rebels, and the Kingdom of Ireland was officially created in 1542 to consolidate English control. It was not a successful strategy and rebellions would occur again and again. Plans to confiscate Irish-owned lands and gift them to English arrivals sparked two separate Desmond Rebellions in Munster in the sixteenth century. These were also crushed with brutal ferocity, Crown general Humphrey Gilbert wishing to strike fear into rebel hearts. He was said to have ordered the following:

> The heads of all those which were killed in the day, should be cut off from their bodies and brought to the place where he incamped at night, and should there be laid on the ground by each side of the way leading into his own tent so that none could come into his tent for any cause but commonly he must pass through a lane of heads.[8]

Another tactic of the English in Munster was scorched earth, where crops were destroyed to ensure the native population would have nothing to eat. Edmund Spenser recounted the result of this tactic:

---

8 Churchyard, T., *A Generall Rehearsall of Warres* (1579)

> Out of every corner of the wood and glens they came creeping forth upon their hands, for their legs could not bear them; they looked anatomies [of] death, they spoke like ghosts crying out of their graves; they did eat of the carrions, happy where they could find them, yea, and one another soon after ... in a short space there were none almost left, and a most populous and plentiful country suddenly left void of man or beast.[9]

A massacre during the second Desmond Rebellion that lives on in infamy occurred in 1580 at Smerwick Harbour, Co. Kerry, one of the most westerly points in Ireland. Both the Spanish and the Pope had agreed to send troops to join the rebels against the English, their sworn enemies. Landing at Kerry, these reinforcements found themselves vastly outnumbered and were shown no mercy. All enemies of the Crown, foreign and Irish, men and women, were killed. Many were beheaded, their heads being dumped in the nearby Gort na gCinn, the field of heads, their bodies being thrown into the sea. More massacres of Spaniards would occur in 1588, when beleaguered soldiers shipwrecked during the Spanish Armada came ashore. The Elizabethan government had issued orders to show no mercy to any Spanish soldier and Richard Bingham, the president of Connacht, followed the queen's command to the letter, executing over a thousand survivors. In one case, 300 members of the crew from a ship that had been wrecked in Galway Bay were taken to a hill above Galway City and beheaded.

By this time, the Crown was also facilitating an informal colonisation of part of the province of Ulster. Thousands of mainly English settlers were pouring into the north, with unsurprising resistance coming from the Irish who resided there. The Rathlin Island massacre on the island off the Antrim coast occurred on 26 July 1575, resulting in the deaths of over 600 Scottish and

---

9 Spenser, E., *A View of the Present State of Ireland* (1970), p.104.

Irish men, women and children who had placed themselves on the island and announced themselves opposed to settlers being forced on Ulster. This destruction is barely imaginable – the population of this small island today is just 140.

The (Bad) Luck of the Irish

Every Irish rebellion seems to have been beset by problems and bad luck and it often seemed like anything that could go wrong, did go wrong. One example was the Nine Years' War, which began in 1593 and which initially saw the Irish achieving some remarkable successes. Red Hugh, a member of the powerful Ulster O'Neill clan, was the instigator. He was imprisoned by the English as a teenager, being considered a threat to their rule, and had made several bold escape attempts, including an ultimately successful effort to achieve freedom by wading through the sewers of Dublin Castle. In the aftermath, O'Neill hid out in the Wicklow Mountains in winter, suffering frostbite and nearly losing his foot. He eventually made his way back to Ulster, where he decided to rebel with the help of neighbouring tribes such as the O'Donnells, led by Hugh Roe O'Donnell. There were some stunning successes. In 1595, their army ambushed an English force in the Curlew Mountains in Co. Roscommon, killing 500 of them. Eventually, the rebels managed to enlist the help of the Spanish under King Philip II. The Spanish king was only too happy to send soldiers to Ireland to deal a blow to his old enemy in England after the horrors inflicted upon Spanish soldiers in the previous decades.

O'Neill and O'Donnell's fight against the English was progressing well in Ulster and beyond, and the thought of 4,800 Spanish soldiers was enough to make them dream of a long-awaited victory. Unfortunately for all but the English, the

Spanish soldiers mistakenly landed in Kinsale, Co. Cork, on the southern coast of Ireland and about as far from Ulster as one can get on the island of Ireland. The Spanish were quickly surrounded by English soldiers in this unfamiliar terrain. O'Neill and O'Donnell's band marched the 250 miles to Kinsale as quickly as they could but were exhausted by the time they arrived. In just an hour, 1,200 Irish soldiers were lost while the English were almost completely unscathed. The loss practically ended the rebellion and would have far-reaching consequences. O'Neill surrendered, and in 1607 many of the most important families of Ulster, fearing retribution, deserted the country in what became known as 'the Flight of the Earls'. Their land would now be ripe for plantation by loyal subjects of the Crown. What might have been if the Spanish had landed at Killybegs, Co. Donegal, instead of Kinsale, Co. Cork? Might the whole future of Irish history have been changed utterly?

English and Scottish planters were then dispatched to Ireland, where they were provided with land that had been seized from the native Irish, something that caused slow-burning and bitter resentment and culminated in the 1641 Rebellion. At this stage, the English Civil War was ongoing, and with few British soldiers to protect the settlers, the massacres that followed live on in infamy for many. The country-wide rebellion was particularly bloody in Ulster, where thousands of settlers were put to the sword. In one witness testimony, Eleanor Price from Co. Armagh recounted how she was captured by rebels, who threw five of her children, as well as other settlers, off a bridge into the River Bann near Portadown. She alleged that most drowned, including several of her children, and that any survivor who made it to shore was killed on the riverbank. The Irish afterwards reclaimed much of the land that had been taken from them in previous decades. They would pay the price in due course. Stories of these massacres of Protestants ringing in his ears, Oliver Cromwell, fresh from winning the

English Civil War against the Royalists, arrived in Ireland with a powerful army behind him and hate in his heart.

On 3 September 1649, Cromwell's forces laid siege to the town of Drogheda, Co. Louth. Over several days, they forced admittance after battering the town's walls with heavy artillery. No one was spared in the subsequent massacre, with an estimated 2,000 people being killed, many brutally and callously while offering no resistance. One month later, having marched his men down the east coast, Wexford town was next and Cromwell's forces massacred thousands here as well. Word of these horrors reached other Irish towns, many of whom surrendered immediately to spare their citizens the terrible death that was likely to await them otherwise. Cromwell's army decimated Ireland, seizing prime farmland and forcing all Catholics or other citizens considered disloyal 'to hell or to Connacht', Connacht being the smallest province with the worst-quality land.

King James II at the Battle of the Boyne. (M. Guizot, *A Popular History of England*, 1850)

Others were sent to the Burren in Co. Clare, derided by one Cromwellian general as being 'a country where there is not water enough to drown a man, wood enough to hang one, nor earth enough to bury him'. Much of the prime land seized was then given to Cromwellian soldiers and their families as a reward for their part in the brutal campaign. In many cases, the descendants of these families would be among the largest landowners in Ireland for centuries.

The War of the Two Kings, when the Catholic King James II was beaten at the Battle of the Boyne in Co. Meath in 1690 by the Protestant William of Orange, also divided Ireland along sectarian lines. When asked by a woman after the battle what had occurred, legend has it that King James II said 'the cowardly Irish ran away'. The woman allegedly replied 'then I see Your Majesty has won the race'. This was one of the last times in history that two kings would personally face off on a battlefield and it was a war that would drain the resistance out of the Irish for several generations.

The Irish were bloodied and bruised and there would be no major uprising for more than 100 years. What followed were the Penal Laws, which left the Catholics of Ireland downtrodden, poor, deprived of education and too dispirited to rebel.

The Penal Laws and 1798

The Penal Laws largely barred priests from practising their ministry in Ireland and forbade the construction of Catholic churches. This forced Catholics to worship in secret at remote Mass Rocks, often located on hillsides across the country. Catholics faced numerous other restrictions: they were barred from voting, prohibited from owning weapons, and not allowed to purchase land from Protestants. In addition, their children were denied access to formal schooling. Despite these oppressive laws, many Catholic parents remained determined to educate their children. As a result, informal hedge schools, led by unofficial schoolmasters, proliferated throughout the country during the eighteenth century. These modest schools offered instruction in reading, writing and arithmetic in exchange for a small fee, playing a crucial role in preserving education in Ireland. They also served as important centres for maintaining Irish history and culture during a time of suppression.

Reflecting on these draconian laws, it is not so much a surprise that the 1798 Rebellion occurred but that no such rebellion had occurred in over a century. This revolt was another case where foreign help could have turned the tide of war, only for some bad luck. The French had earlier agreed to aid any Irish rebellion and sent some 14,000 soldiers to Ireland in forty-three ships. There was a two-month delay in their departure, however, and they could not leave until just before Christmas 1796, in one of the stormiest winters in years. At Bantry Bay, Co. Cork, a huge gale struck, making landing impossible. They rerouted north to Co. Sligo. On the way there, however, they were struck by more hurricane-force winds, several vessels being destroyed. The remaining ships turned tail for France, scuppering a golden opportunity to catch Crown forces unawares. Some 1,500 men were lost in what turned out to be an utterly pointless venture. This made it even more surprising when a rebellion exploded into life in May 1798. Several early victories in Co. Wexford, and simultaneous uprisings in Co. Antrim and Down, gave the Irish hope that they might be able to force change, despite their lack of weaponry.

The rebellion is remembered for its savagery and every engagement had horrific consequences for one side or another. One massacre committed by the Irish occurred at Scullabogue in Co. Wexford in 1798. As the rebellion was intensifying, people considered to be from loyalist families, most of them

Protestant men, women and children, were taken forcibly to a barn at Scullabogue, where they were interned. When their guards heard about British atrocities that had occurred in nearby New Ross, their response was to burn the barn with everyone inside it. There were likely to have been 100 people burned to death in the incident. This seemingly sectarian massacre is puzzling in light of the fact that many of the leaders of the United Irishmen, most notably Wolfe Tone, were from Protestant backgrounds. The Crown was also utterly without mercy and the United Irishmen were ultimately defeated after brutal tactics, such as half-hanging, pitch-capping (where hot tar is poured onto the head) and mass executions, were used to force the surrender of the poorly armed rebels. One example of many was the horrific death suffered by Fr John Murphy, one of the rebel leaders. He was first tortured in an effort to obtain more information about his fellow rebels before he was stripped, flogged, hanged and decapitated. In a final act of savagery, his body was burned in a barrel of tar and his head placed on a spike. Wolfe Tone also died, his throat cut in prison, but whether this was a self-inflicted wound or one committed by a captor will never be fully known.

The British wished to ensure that no such rebellion would occur again. In 1782, Ireland had been given some form of legislative independence in the form of Grattan's parliament, which lasted almost two decades but barred Catholics from sitting. After 1798, the British no longer felt like an Irish parliament was a good idea. Unbelievably, the British coerced the members of the Irish parliament to vote itself out of existence, something that would allow the Act of Union to unite England, Scotland, Ireland and Wales and place Ireland once again fully and firmly under the control of Westminster. The United Kingdom was thus born in 1801. There would be another rebellion in 1803, led by Robert Emmet, but it would be a dismal failure, although the Chief Justice of Ireland, Lord Kilwarden, was taken from his coach and killed. Kilwarden had been the prosecutor when United Irishman William Orr was sentenced to death just before the 1798 Rebellion, and was thus considered a legitimate target by Emmet's men. Emmet himself was horrified by the violence, however. He went into hiding but was swiftly captured and found guilty of high treason. He famously said from the dock:

> Let no man write my epitaph, for as no man who knows my motives dare now vindicate them, let not prejudice or ignorance asperse them. Let them and me rest in obscurity and peace, and my tomb remain uninscribed. When my country takes her place among the nations of the earth, then let my epitaph be written.[10]

As an example to any other would-be rebels, Emmet was hanged and beheaded publicly as a traitor. He was buried in a pauper's grave initially, but his body was later taken by sympathetic friends. The mystery begins at this point for, despite many theories, it is unknown to this day where Emmet was reinterred. His wish for his grave to remain unmarked came true, and although his country has now taken its place among the nations of the Earth, it seems likely to remain that way.

---

10 Guiney, L., *Robert Emmet* (1904), p.54.

5

Crime, Punishment and Disaster in Irish History

Strange Irish Murders

Crime has been a feature of society for as long as humans have walked the earth and there have been some strange and unbelievable misdemeanours in the annals of Irish history. The murder of the Colleen Bawn is one crime that continues to fascinate, centuries after it occurred. Cailín Bán comes from the Irish words for 'fair girl', a name that was posthumously given to Limerick woman Ellen Scanlan (née Hanley). She was only 15 years old, and famed for her beauty, when she was murdered in 1819. The murder was committed at the behest of her new husband, John Scanlan, of Bruff, Co. Limerick. Scanlan was a member of the ascendency who had married Ellen despite his being from a far more prosperous family than she. His family did not approve of the match and, having grown tired of his wife after just weeks of marriage, he convinced his bungling servant Stephen Sullivan to bring Ellen out onto the River Shannon on a boat and kill her. Sullivan did this by shooting her with a musket and beating her, in a murder attempt he nearly botched. He then dumped her body in the water, although it would later wash up near Kilrush in Co. Clare. The body was identified and a manhunt was begun. Scanlan had fled the scene and changed his name but was eventually apprehended, tried and found guilty, despite being defended by politician Daniel O'Connell. He was hanged in Co. Clare, as was Sullivan, who had also fled before being apprehended. The murder captured the Irish imagination and has been adapted into several plays. It was even made into an early silent film in 1911.

Another particularly bizarre crime was the 1871 murder of William Glass, an official at the Northern Bank in the small town of Newtownstewart in Co. Tyrone. Glass was brutally beaten and had a file put through his skull in the bank in broad daylight, with £1,600 then stolen. The most chilling aspect of the crime was the perpetrator. Brendan Behan once said that he had never seen a situation so dismal that a policeman could not make it worse, and in this case the policeman tasked with investigating the killing, Sub-Inspector Thomas Hartley Montgomery, came under suspicion when colleagues noted his increasingly bizarre methods of 'solving' the crime. After three lengthy trials, the policeman was finally found guilty. Despite denying any part in the crime during the trial, he made a confession before his execution, describing himself as quite mad, although a more mundane explanation was the policeman's desire for money to ease the financial difficulties he was experiencing. He had been a close friend of Glass's in life, making the case all the more horrifying. Montgomery was executed by hanging in Omagh Gaol on 26 August 1873.

A Crime Committed?

One of the most enduring mysteries in the annals of Irish crime occurred on Christmas Day, 1929, when Larry Griffin, a postman from Kilmacthomas, Co. Waterford, disappeared after completing his rounds in the nearby village of Stradbally. Griffin had been invited in for glasses of whiskey in several houses throughout the day and it appeared that he had entered Whelan's Pub to continue his carousing that evening. He did not return home that night, and his bicycle was found lying on the road 2 miles away early the next morning, looking suspiciously like it had been carefully placed there. Despite extensive searches over the next few months, Griffin was never found. A witness, Jim Fitzgerald, later claimed the postman was killed in Whelan's Pub after an altercation with a local labourer, and his body was hidden, possibly down a local mine, by several prominent local members of the community, including a school teacher and two Gardaí, who had driven it away in the village's only motor car. This had been done, apparently, to protect everyone in the pub, who should not have been there on Christmas Day due to the strict licensing laws that forbade pubs opening on that day. However, Fitzgerald later recanted his evidence, and no further proof could be found to support the claim. Ten local people were ultimately tried for concealing the body, but the case was dismissed. Griffin's disappearance remains unsolved to this day.

The theft of the Irish Crown Jewels is another strange mystery that may never be solved. These jewels were worn at ceremonies at which important Irish members were being admitted into the Order of St Patrick. Designed in 1831, the jewels were immensely valuable objects, studded with precious stones such as diamonds, emeralds and rubies. Since that time, they had spent most of their life in a bank vault, before being moved to Dublin Castle in 1903. Here, they were supposed to be placed in a strongroom with several locks that had to be opened to gain admittance, but they ended up in the library as the safe was too wide to fit through the door. Nevertheless, the safe had only two keys and it seemed a relatively secure location. Astonishingly, the jewels were found to be missing on 6 July 1907, although the last time they had definitively been seen was nearly a month earlier. This was a major embarrassment as King Edward VII was due to visit Dublin later in the year.

There was no sign of forced entry and, as the entrance to Dublin Castle was guarded constantly, there was puzzlement as to how someone could have entered the castle and opened the safe. An antiquarian named Arthur Vicars had been in charge of the jewels and he was said to have been careless in his duties. At an earlier stage, they had been stolen as a prank and returned to him in the post. A huge reward elicited no valuable information. How were the jewels disposed of? And more importantly, who took them? One outlandish theory was that the jewels had been stolen by Francis Shackleton, brother of the famous explorer Ernest, after he had got Vicars drunk and taken the key as he lay in a drunken stupor. He had then sold them on the Continent. Shackleton denied this until his death and Vicars was later killed by the IRA in the War of Independence. What became of the Irish Crown Jewels remains a mystery.

Outrageous Irish Criminals Abroad

One crime that is uniquely associated with the nineteenth century was body snatching. At the time, anatomists were eager to find out the inner workings of the human body. For this, they needed corpses to dissect, but few were willing to donate their body to medical science after death. Instead, corpses were often covertly taken from graves and sold on to the anatomists, who rarely asked too many questions as to where they had come from. Bully's Acre, a paupers' gravesite near Kilmainham, Co. Dublin, was one place that was often raided for fresh bodies. The most famous incident of Irish body snatching did not occur on the island of Ireland, however. It was the murders committed by William Burke and William Hare in Edinburgh that live on in infamy, two centuries after they were committed.

Burke was a native of Tyrone who deserted his wife in Ireland to come to Scotland, eventually becoming acquainted with William Hare, also a native of the north of Ireland. Burke and his common-law wife moved into Hare's lodgings in a tenement flat in Edinburgh while the pair occasionally worked as navvies on the Union Canal. This casual labour did not pay well, and Hare also rented out the lodgings at a very low rate to others of little means. In November 1827, one of his lodgers, known as Old Donald, died of dropsy, owing Hare several weeks of unpaid rent. Hare wished to recoup this debt and he conspired with Burke to take Old Donald's body from the coffin, fill the casket with bark, and sell the body on to an anatomist named Dr Knox to earn the money he was owed. Knox asked few questions of the men, such was his enthusiasm for cadavers, and they were delighted to receive more than £7. An assistant of the anatomist even said to the men as they left that they would be happy to see Burke and Hare again if they had another body to dispose of.

The men thus decided that any tenants who died could be disposed of similarly. Unfortunately, they were too impatient to wait for natural deaths to occur. Instead, they turned to murder. Some of their victims were lodgers at Hare's house, while others were invited to the house, incapacitated by alcohol and killed as they lay in a drunken stupor. The bodies were packed into boxes and swiftly brought to the anatomist. In total, the two Irishmen killed sixteen people in the space of twelve months. Burke and Hare were eventually captured when lodgers returned unexpectedly to find a dead body lying in the front room. They reported it to the police, who came to the house to find that the body had already been sold on to Dr Knox. The murderers were arrested and, faced with irrefutable evidence, turned on one another. Hare's evidence was ultimately used to convict his former partner in crime and Burke was hanged in January 1829 in front of 20,000 spectators. His body, appropriately enough, was publicly dissected afterwards. Incredibly, Hare, whom many believed to be the more guilty and less remorseful of the pair, was released on account of giving this evidence, and his whereabouts were never disclosed. Did he return to the land of his birth? We may never know.

Their names lived on in infamy in Scotland and Ireland, however, and several poems were written at the time lamenting their actions. One includes the following verses:

> O Burke, cruel man, how detested thy name is!
> Thy dark deeds of blood are a stain on our times.
> O savage, relentless, forever infamous,
> Long, long will the world remember thy crimes.
>
> Let their guilt and their gloom speak of nothing but terror,
> Some dark deeds of blood to the stranger declare,
> And ages to come ever mark them with horror,
> For the ghosts of the murdered will still gather there.[11]

Another astonishing crime abroad was committed by the former national tennis champion Vere Goold. Goold, a member of a prominent Waterford family, had won the Irish national title in 1879 before making the final of the Wimbledon Championship in the same year. Reportedly hungover, Goold had lost this game but was still well known in his homeland after his exploits. This was the high point of Goold's tennis career, as he afterwards became an alcoholic, a gambler and an opium addict. He married Frenchwoman Marie Giraudin, although the pair were continually in debt. Goold's answer was to move to Monte Carlo, where he unleashed a plan to win big at the roulette tables, with predictable results.

A wealthy Danish widow named Emma Levin befriended the impoverished aristocrats and in 1907 she lent them a hefty

---

11 Mac Gregor, G., *The History of Burke and Hare* (1884), p.292.

1,000 francs. The Goolds spent the money, or perhaps gambled it away, and when Levin arrived to their flat in Monte Carlo to reclaim the loan in August 1907, the pair murdered and dismembered her before stuffing her body into a trunk, bringing it to Marseilles railway station and labelling it 'Charing Cross, London', asking that it be dispatched there. They then left quickly. The odour and the blood seeping out of the suitcase aroused suspicions and the case was opened by a porter, who was horrified by the contents. He immediately informed the police and the Goolds were traced to a nearby hotel and arrested. Vere gave a fake name but his identity was quickly discovered. This news caused a sensation in Ireland, many remembering the charismatic tennis star of years before. Vere Goold was tried and found guilty of the murder, although prosecutors insisted that his wife was the main architect of the murderous plan. She was sentenced to be guillotined, but reprieved, whereas Goold was dispatched to the infamous Devil's Island Prison where, suffering from opium and alcohol withdrawal, he committed suicide a year later.

Lizzie Halliday, born Elizabeth McNally in Co. Antrim, showed that it was not just men from Ireland who were capable of committing despicable murders abroad. She lived much of her life in New York State, where she murdered at least two of her husbands, as well as two other women who had befriended her. She was also suspected of being involved in several other deaths and was described by newspapers at the time as the most evil woman on Earth. In 1894, Halliday became the first woman to be sentenced to death in the electric chair, but was pardoned by the state governor on account of her sex and her questionable mental state. She went on to stab a nurse to death in the mental institution in which she was housed and was ever after kept under lock and key, sometimes chained to the floor. She died in 1918, at which point she was buried in an unmarked grave.

Irish Pirates, Outlaws and Highwaymen

Piracy was common in Ireland in the sixteenth century, much of it spearheaded by a woman named Gráinne Ní Mháille (Grace O'Malley.) Born on Clare Island, Co. Mayo, in 1530, Grace was nicknamed Gráinne Mhaol (Bald Grace) after cutting her own hair short as a young child in order to be able to look like a boy and join her father's seafaring expeditions. She proved herself an able sailor and travelled all over Europe. At the age of 16, she married Donal of the neighbouring O'Flaherty tribe, who had previously been sworn enemies of the O'Malleys, a union that further added to her wealth and notoriety. When Grace's father died, she assumed control of his whole fleet, which was able to control much of Ireland's west coast. She sailed to many countries, trading all sorts of goods. Many of the tactics used to gain control of the sea were not strictly legal and Grace earned another nickname: the Pirate Queen. Her husband was killed in battle in 1565. After this, Grace married another powerful chieftain, Richard Bourke, and continued to fight many battles against neighbouring tribes and against English law and order. Richard Bingham was appointed president of Connacht in 1584 and was determined to bring the province under control. At one session in Galway in 1586, he put seventy people to death. He was also a sworn enemy of Gráinne Mhaol. She requested and was granted a meeting with Queen Elizabeth I to complain about his arrest of her family members. Grace would not bow to Elizabeth, believing herself to be a queen and an equal of the English monarch. Nevertheless, Elizabeth must have been impressed by her visitor as she agreed to return many of Grace's titles and some of her land. Grace continued her life at sea until her death in 1603.

Another formidable Irish female pirate was Anne Bonny, who was born in Co. Cork but moved to South Carolina at a young age.

In 1718, Anne married a sailor named John Bonny and the couple travelled to the Bahamas, where Anne became involved with a pirate named Calico Jack. She helped her new beau seize the sloop *William* and they began pirating merchant vessels in the Caribbean. A woman on a pirate ship was unusual at the time but Anne was said to have possessed a fierce nature. She did not hide her sex from her crewmates, but occasionally disguised herself as a man when raiding or participating in combat. Bonny was eventually arrested for her crimes, although she put up fierce resistance, and was found guilty and sentenced to death. Her pregnancy saved her life and her sentence was commuted. Anne was eventually released from prison, returning to South Carolina where she lived out her life peacefully.

Ireland itself suffered from pirate attacks occasionally, most notably in the summer of 1631 when the Cork maritime village of Baltimore experienced a sensational raid. Two Algerian ships arrived at the village on 19 June, although among the pirates were European renegades. They attacked under the cover of darkness and the inhabitants were completely taken off guard. Two hundred or so raiders set homes alight before marching perhaps a hundred villagers from their beds and taking them to the waiting ships. Most appear to have been taken to Africa, where they were used as concubines or sold as slaves and few, if any, ever saw their homeland again.

There are also many well-known outlaws internationally with Irish roots. The character Zorro was said to be based on Wexford man William Lamport, who was executed in Mexico for his efforts to foment rebellion against the Spanish Crown. Equally famous is Ned Kelly, the son of Irish emigrant John 'Red' Kelly, one of thousands of Irish people transported to the Australian penal colony. In his case, it was for the stealing of two pigs. Born in Australia in 1855, his son Ned went on to be 'a rambling gambler', in his own words. His first brush with the law was in 1869 when he robbed a Chinese hawker named Ah Fook of

Billy the Kid. (Emerson Hough, *The Story of the Outlaw*, 1907)

Ned Kelly. (Francis Hare, *The Last of the Bushrangers*, 1892)

10 shillings. Kelly's exploits escalated and he and his gang would regularly steal horses in the coming years. More seriously, he was accused of shooting and injuring a policeman named Fitzpatrick, who had come to his home to arrest his brother, Dan, for horse theft in 1877. Ned and his brother fled and were wanted men thereafter. The Kellys' mother was arrested and imprisoned for the attack on the policeman in their absence, something that enraged Ned. He formed the Kelly Gang and, seeking refuge from the law, began to rob banks, distil illicit whiskey and find other ways to finance the gang's existence.

Police finally came upon the gang at Stringybark Creek the following year but three men of the law were killed in the shootout, Ned Kelly escaping unharmed. The gang again fled but there was now a massive manhunt against them and an £8,000 reward offered for their capture. They managed to rob several more banks over the next eighteen months, staying out of reach of the authorities with the help of a large network of sympathisers. Kelly generally treated anyone caught up in the robberies well and wrote a famous letter in which he explained his actions and listed the alleged injustices he and his family had suffered from the police. The letter also mentioned his pride in his Irish heritage and the long history of Irish rebellions against the English. Kelly was finally captured after a shootout with the police in Glenrowan, Victoria, in 1880. He was tried by an Irish judge, Redmond Barry, but he had little sympathy for the outlaw. Kelly was found guilty of the murder of one of the policemen at Stringybark Creek and was executed later that year, despite a widely signed petition and large protests. His last words were said to have been 'Such is life.' Kelly's body was placed in a wooden box and dumped into a mass grave with those of other prisoners. His legacy remains divisive, many viewing him as a champion of the underprivileged, others seeing him as a criminal whose reckless actions led to the death of three policemen. His name is remembered in Ireland. For several years, the village of Moyglass in Tipperary hosted a Ned Kelly festival, and a song titled 'The Ballad of Kelly's Gang', set to the tune of 'The Wearing of the Green', was once sung widely throughout that county. In 2001, Ned Kelly was even commemorated on an Irish postage stamp.

Billy the Kid was another outlaw with strong Irish heritage. Born in an Irish neighbourhood in New York City to Irish parents, Catherine Devine and Patrick McCarty, some accounts even state that Henry McCarty, later known as Billy the Kid, was an Irish speaker. Either way, he grew to epitomise the Wild West, where he became a notorious member of the group of outlaws known as the Regulators. Billy the Kid killed numerous men in his twenty-one years and was sentenced to be hanged after shooting a county sheriff dead. Sensationally, he managed to escape from custody by freeing himself from his handcuffs and killing two sheriffs' deputies. He evaded capture for two further months despite an enormous manhunt. He was finally shot dead by Sheriff Pat Garrett, also of Irish descent, in New Mexico Territory in 1881.

Irish Highwaymen

Ireland had plenty of outlaws in its own land, in the form of highwaymen. In the seventeenth century these highwaymen were called 'tories' (from the Irish word for raider), though they later became widely known as 'rapparees'. These men often came from the dispossessed Irish class, whose lands had been seized during the plantations, and they typically targeted English planters and the gentry, acts that often won them support among the native Irish. One notable rapparee was 'Black Francis' McHugh from Tyrone, whose band once stole 70,000 gold sovereigns from redcoats. McHugh was eventually captured near Enniskillen in 1780. At his trial, the daughter of a

house he had plundered pleaded for mercy for McHugh due to his respectful conduct, but he was hanged nonetheless. The only thing worse than being hanged is being hanged twice, as Patrick O'Brien of Loughrea, Co. Galway, found out after being found guilty of highway robbery in England. After the hanging, he was cut down and his friends claimed his body. As they travelled to the graveyard, they noticed that he was not in fact dead. O'Brien fully recovered and, after a brief spell making an honest living, he returned to crime and was involved in a murder. Arrested once again near Salisbury, he was executed for a second time, this time wrapped in iron chains, in April 1689.

O'Brien was not the only Irish highwaymen to ply his trade in England, nor the only one to be hanged there. James Maclaine, the so-called 'gentleman highwayman', was born in 1724 in Co. Monaghan to a Presbyterian minister. When sent to procure an education in Dublin, he instead squandered his inheritance on gambling and fine clothes before moving to England, where he married. When his wife died after two years, he turned to highway robbery with an Irish accomplice named William Plunkett. They held up travellers around London, including the politician Horace Walpole in 1749. Walpole was the son of the first British Prime Minister, Sir Robert Walpole, and this caused Maclaine's notoriety to grow. A botched robbery in 1750 led to his arrest after he was found attempting to sell the stolen goods. He was swiftly tried and hanged at Tyburn.

One highwayman who was blessed with a more peaceful end was James Freney, known widely as 'Freney the Robber'. Like Maclaine, the Kilkenny native came from a respectable background but he was more interested in hurling, drinking and gambling than work, and mounting debts pushed him into crime. He robbed the wealthy on roads, often with a pistol and a swift horse, and sometimes broke into homes. Despite his crimes, Freney was widely seen as gallant and charitable and, in one story, he gave a large amount of gold to a widow who had fed him while he was in hiding. Declared an outlaw in 1749, Freney surrendered and avoided execution by being exiled. He returned to Ireland and later published a successful autobiography in 1754, ironically ending his days as a customs official in New Ross, Co. Wexford. He died in 1788, unusually old for a highwayman, but in his lifetime he was believed to have buried valuable treasure on Brandon Hill, about 2 miles from Graiguenamanagh. If so, it has yet to be discovered.

Miscarriage of Justice?

Not all murders have a clear-cut perpetrator and, in some cases, we cannot even be sure if a murder took place at all, as in the case of Maria Kirwan.

Ireland's Eye is a small uninhabited island off North County Dublin, popular with day trippers. On 6 September 1852, the renowned painter William Burke Kirwan travelled by boat with his wife Maria to the island on a painting expedition. When the boatmen who had brought the pair out returned that evening to collect them, William told them that he had not seen his wife in some time. They searched the island, only to find Maria drowned in a shallow pool. Although it was initially accepted that she had died accidentally, suspicion began to mount against the artist when he displayed some rather odd behaviour after his wife's death. He insisted that her body should be immediately washed and cleaned, despite numerous locals telling him to wait for an inquest. Rumours also began to spread that Kirwan had kept a mistress for many years and the pair had several children together, something that seemed to provide him with a motive. In addition, several people came forward stating that they had heard screaming from the mainland across the narrow channel to the island earlier in the day. Kirwan was eventually arrested and stood trial in December 1852, where the jury heard about unexplained cuts and marks on Maria's body and William's wet clothes after the incident. The defence insisted that Maria had suffered an epileptic fit and drowned. Regardless, Kirwan was found guilty of murder. He spent twenty-seven years in prison, although he never admitted to any part in the crime, if indeed a crime had been committed. He was released in 1879 and was said to have emigrated to America to join his lover, but not before making one last trip to Ireland's Eye. He died shortly afterwards. The question remains: was a murder committed on Ireland's Eye? We may never know. Burke Kirwan's paintings remain in the National Library of Ireland to this day, including one of the Martello Tower on Ireland's Eye and another of Maria Kirwan, his tragic wife.

In some cases, we can be sure that a grave injustice has occurred. In Ireland, the two most famous miscarriages of justice are undoubtedly the unrelated hangings of Myles Joyce and Harry Gleeson. In Joyce's case, the tragic chain of events began on the night of 17 August 1882, when a group of men broke into the home of John Joyce in Maamtrasna, a rural mountainous townland in Co. Galway. Within minutes, a horrific massacre unfolded. John Joyce, his wife Bridget, his elderly mother Margaret (aged 80), his daughter Peggy and his son Michael were all brutally murdered. One son, Patsy, survived, despite sustaining serious injuries. The government believed that the crime had an agrarian motive and ten local men were quickly arrested. Most spoke only Irish but were tried individually in English. The first three to stand trial, Pat Casey, Pat Joyce and Myles Joyce, pleaded not guilty.

Nevertheless, they were convicted and sentenced to death, largely on the basis of highly questionable eyewitness testimony. Two of the ten defendants turned state evidence, giving testimony they later recanted, while the five others received long prison terms. Just days before the execution date, Pat Casey and

Pat Joyce submitted written statements incriminating themselves and clearing Myles Joyce, insisting he was not involved in the murders. Joyce had maintained his innocence from the beginning and he expected a pardon to follow these exonerating statements. The staff at Galway Gaol stayed up through the night in anticipation of a reprieve. But no pardon came. Just before his death, Joyce proclaimed, 'Tá mé chomh neamhchiontach leis an leanbh sa chliabhán' ('I am as innocent as the child in the cradle'). His final words before his execution were 'Cén fáth mé chur ann báis?' ('Why am I being put to death?') Despite this, he was hanged, leaving behind a wife and five children. It was not until 2018 that he was formally pardoned. In 2021, another man named John Twiss was exonerated. He had been hanged on flimsy evidence for an agrarian murder in Co. Cork in 1895, leaving one to wonder how many others had been convenient scapegoats for crimes in nineteenth-century Ireland.

It was due to cases like this that many thought Ireland would abolish the death penalty when it became independent in 1922, but, with a looming civil war, it was retained. This was a decision that was not welcomed by all, many viewing the penalty negatively due to the execution of many Irish fighters in the Easter Rising and War of Independence. Twenty-nine hangings of murderers would occur until the noose was used for the last time in 1954. Undoubtedly the most notorious of these was the hanging of Harry Gleeson in 1941 for the murder of his neighbour, Moll McCarthy, in New Inn, Co. Tipperary, the previous November. Moll had given birth to children from several fathers and there were many potential suspects, but it was the prosecution's case that Harry was the father of her most recent child, something there was no evidence to support. The trial was unsatisfactory and subsequent examination of the case shows a conspiracy of sorts against the unfortunate Gleeson. The real perpetrators were said to be powerful members of the local community who used Gleeson as an easy scapegoat.

Gleeson went to his death despite being completely innocent of the despicable crime. After many years of pressure, Gleeson was finally exonerated in 2015.

Interestingly, Ireland never trained its own official executioner. Instead, the government relied on a series of English hangmen to carry out the grim duty. Among the most frequently employed were members of the Pierrepoint family, a well-known dynasty of British executioners. Their arrival in Ireland was often met with hostility. Crowds gathered at the docks to jeer and hiss as they stepped off the boat and Albert Pierrepoint later revealed that he carried a gun in his pocket during his visits to Ireland, so intense was the local resentment. At one stage, the IRA even plotted to kidnap Pierrepoint, and might have succeeded had they intercepted him en route to the execution chamber at Mountjoy Prison. The idea of an Englishman being paid by the Irish state to hang Irish citizens sat uneasily with many, regardless of the fact that those facing the gallows were often guilty of appalling crimes.

Political Crimes

Ireland has also seen its fair share of political crimes. The most famous is undoubtedly the Phoenix Park Murders, when the Chief Secretary of Ireland, Lord Frederick Cavendish, was set upon and stabbed to death in broad daylight in the famous Dublin park on 6 May 1882. His under-secretary Thomas Burke, the target of the attack, was also killed. This was the most high-profile assassination in recent Irish history and it made news headlines all over the world. Cavendish was a close friend of the Prime Minister, William Gladstone, and related to him through marriage, and the British public clamoured for the assassins to be brought to justice. The police spared no resources in catching the assailants, who came from a secret society known as the Invincibles. No fewer than five of their number were hanged for the crime, mainly on the evidence of an informer from within their ranks, James Carey. Carey was a hate figure in Dublin in the aftermath and was bundled onto a ship bound for South Africa and given a new name. Unfortunately for him, he was recognised by a fellow passenger, Donegal man Patrick O'Donnell, who shot Carey dead while on board the ship. O'Donnell was brought to London and hanged in 1883, bringing the fatality count of this crime and its aftermath to nine men. Another assassination that came close to this in terms of outrage was the shooting of Kevin O'Higgins, the Minister for Justice, in 1927. O'Higgins was shot by three IRA men who had been on the opposite side in the civil war, and who held him responsible for the execution policy enacted by the state during that conflict. These men were never convicted, although their identity has come to light in recent years.

The most famous Irish politician of the first half of the nineteenth century, Daniel O'Connell, often told his followers that freedom was not worth one drop of Irish blood. His pacifism stemmed from his time in Paris, where he saw the violent excesses of the French Revolution with his own eyes. Less well known is the fact that O'Connell spilled some blood himself when he killed a man named John D'Esterre in a duel in 1815. The duel came about as O'Connell had insulted Dublin Corporation in a political speech and D'Esterre, a corporation member, demanded his words be withdrawn. O'Connell did not do so and D'Esterre upped the stakes, publicly demanding a duel. O'Connell ignored the offer initially but, after repeated accusations of being a coward, decided to accept it. O'Connell was a good shot for a pacifist and the duel was arranged for Bishops' Court, Co. Kildare, with both men being armed with pistols. Each man was limited to one shot. A large crowd watched as D'Esterre took aim and fired first. His shot was wide of the mark. O'Connell returned fire and hit his rival in the groin. The bullet went on to lodge in the base of D'Esterre's spine, causing him an agonising death. O'Connell was wracked with guilt and agreed to provide an allowance to his vanquished foe's daughter, something that was paid regularly until his own death more than thirty years later. O'Connell did not immediately turn against violence, and almost became embroiled in another duel with the soon-to-be British prime minister, Robert Peel, shortly afterwards. He was arrested on his way to the duel and he eventually became more steadfast in his absolute abhorrence for violence. He did not contest a duel again.

O'Connell was not even the only Irish member of parliament who killed someone in a duel, a popular method of solving quarrels in Ireland before the 1820s. Richard Martin, born in 1754, was an extensive landholder and member of parliament for Co. Galway. Widely remembered as an animal rights campaigner who was nicknamed 'Humanity Dick' after he helped to set up the Royal Society for the Prevention of Cruelty to Animals, Martin had a second nickname: Hair-trigger Dick. This was due to his penchant for duelling. In 1785, Martin had a public spat with his cousin James Jordan over an insulting remark he was alleged to have made. Jordan challenged him to a duel, which Richard reluctantly accepted. Jordan was shot dead in the duel and, much like O'Connell, Martin regretted this for the rest of his life.

Irish Disasters on Land and Sea

Over the centuries, Ireland has experienced numerous disasters resulting in significant loss of life. One such tragedy took place on 4 September 1828, when around thirty-one people boarded an old wooden boat at Annaghdown Pier in Co. Galway to travel

A memorial to the *Lusitania* in Cobh, Co. Cork. (Photograph by the author)

the 8 miles to a fair in Galway City via Lough Corrib. Along with the passengers, the boat carried sheep and various goods for sale. Struggling under the heavy load, the vessel began to falter, possibly due to a sheep putting its hoof through a plank, allowing water to flood in. Despite the courageous rescue efforts of some passengers, at least nineteen lives were lost.

The sinking of both *Lusitania* and *Titanic* also had strong Irish connections. *Lusitania*, torpedoed by a German U-boat in 1915 when it was just 12 miles off the coast of Co. Cork, sank rapidly, leading to the loss of nearly 1,200 lives. There were approximately 140 Irish people on board. Many of the bodies recovered were brought ashore to Cobh, the nearest port to the sinking, and buried there. The town now has a memorial and museum dedicated to the tragedy. Cobh was also inextricably linked with the sinking of the Belfast-built *Titanic*, it being the last port the ship visited before it struck an iceberg in the north Atlantic. Once again, over 100 of *Titanic*'s passengers were Irish, many of whom perished in the icy waters.

Another deadly Irish maritime tragedy was the sudden powerful storm that struck the west coast on 28 October 1927. It led to huge loss of life, both in the area around Lacken and the Inishkea Islands off Co. Mayo, and further south at Cleggan Bay and Inishbofin Island in Galway. Hundreds of fishermen were out at sea in their small traditional currachs when the storm struck and many were unable to return to shore. In the end, twenty-five fishermen from the Galway fishing communities of Rossadillisk, near Cleggan, and Inishbofin Island lost their lives, while twenty Mayo fisherman suffered similar fates. Many of the bodies were never recovered. This disaster was one among numerous maritime tragedies, many of which deeply impacted the small island communities along the coast and would lead indirectly to the desertion of the Inishkea islands several years later and the relocation of its people on to the nearby mainland.

The Dromcollogher cinema fire occurred just twelve months before, on 5 September 1926, and it proved to be one of the most destructive tragedies in modern Ireland. It was a Sunday night and hundreds crowded into an upstairs loft in a barn near the village to watch a showing of Cecil B. DeMille's *The Ten Commandments*. The reel had been brought from Cork City, where cinemas were closed on Sundays, and set up in the shed. This practice was against the law, but with money to be made providing makeshift cinemas in rural villages, this law was regularly flouted. A generator powered the reel but candles were lit around the projector to provide extra light. Midway through the film, one of these candles fell and set the highly flammable film reels on fire. Soon, the barn was ablaze. Those lucky enough to be beside the doors escaped. The ladder down from the loft became a scene of carnage and some jumped down a floor to make their way to safety. Others smashed the window upstairs to escape. Several people made their way to freedom this way until one woman got caught in the window and could not be pushed out or in. With fire spreading quickly, many began to suffer the effects of smoke inhalation. Ultimately, forty-eight people died in what remains one of the worst tragedies in Irish history. The number of dead was exactly equalled in the Stardust Tragedy of 1981, however. A nightclub in Artane, Dublin, the venue was popular with young people and there was strict security to ensure that no one could gain entrance without paying. Exits were chained and this made it difficult to escape when the fire started. The findings of the subsequent investigation were met with fury by the victims' families and the state finally issued a public apology for its handling of this tragedy in 2024.

In 1937, another fire that took the lives of Irish people happened in Kirkintilloch, Scotland, although all the dead were natives of the area around Achill Island in Co. Mayo. This area had a long-standing reliance on 'tattie hoking' or seasonal labour, where hundreds of Achill Islanders would travel to Scotland to do various jobs, especially potato picking. The extra money from these jobs was brought home and used to pay the rent and feed the family for the remainder of the year. The living conditions were often rudimentary, and in Kirkintilloch their lodgings were in a shed with a sliding door fastened from the outside by a padlock to keep the workers in at night. The windows also had wire netting on the outside, making it impossible to escape when fire engulfed the shed in the early hours of 16 September 1937. Figures were seen through the window attempting to escape, as desperate attempts to force open the shed door failed. The foreman with the key for the padlock could not be found for some time and when the door was finally opened, the bodies of the ten occupants, all boys and men aged between 13 and 23 years, were discovered. Achill's railway link to Westport was discontinued in 1937. Its final journey would carry the bodies of many of the victims of the Kirkintilloch fire to their final resting place.

This was not the first tragedy to strike the tattie hokers of Achill. On 14 June 1894, thirty-two people were drowned when a ship bringing them on the first leg of their journey to Scotland capsized near Westport. The news reached Achill swiftly, and newspapers reported scenes of overwhelming sorrow, some families losing as many as three members. The railway line, which had just opened between Westport and Achill, saw its first use: transporting the thirty-two bodies back home. These two events fulfilled a chilling seventeenth-century prophecy by Brian Rua O'Cearbhain, who had predicted that 'carts on iron wheels' would carry dead bodies into Achill on their first and last journey. Donations poured in from across Ireland and beyond, as the tragedy cast a harsh light on the desperate conditions faced by those in the west of Ireland. The *Freeman's Journal* newspaper expressed particular sorrow over the harsh existence endured by people in remote communities like Achill:

> A more industrious people could not be found under heaven. Their toil and thrift would purchase them comfort anywhere except on the melancholy Irish coast to which they cling with a love that wretchedness cannot destroy. They are bound to these shores and even in exile, turn back to them.[12]

The same might be said about the people of Ballymanus, a rural area in Co. Donegal, which was afflicted by a tragedy of similarly horrific proportions. On 10 May 1943, a mysterious object was seen floating in the sea. Dozens of locals flocked to the nearest beach to get a closer look, as many valuable items of flotsam such as rubber, timber and even rum had floated onto Irish shores in the years of the Second World War. This strange item, too, eventually floated onto shore. Locals initially kept their distance, unsure of what it was, but after a time some of the younger men grew brave and began to approach the item. It was a mine and it exploded without warning, obliterating

12 *Freeman's Journal*, 15 June 1894.

those nearest it and knocking unconscious those further away. It was said that the blast could be heard in Derry, 70 miles away, and that the windows of houses up to a mile away were broken by the impact. Nineteen young men between the ages of 14 and 34 died, a lost generation for the small village.

Other Disasters

The worst railway accident in Irish history occurred near Armagh City in June 1889. Most passengers were on a day trip to the seaside organised by the Abbey Street Sunday School and the excursion, costing just 10p, proved popular. The train quickly became overcrowded, with people even sitting in the luggage compartment. There was some worry among staff about the train's ability to safely carry the number of passengers on board and it left fifteen minutes after its scheduled time. Some 3 miles outside Armagh, their fears were realised when the train stalled at the top of a hill. The crew decided to divide the train and bring forward several of the carriages at the front, leaving the rear carriages behind, planning to return for them. The carriages at the back did not have powerful enough brakes, however, and they began to roll, then hurtle, backwards down the track. The panicked passengers threw small children out of the top windows in anticipation of the inevitable collision, which came with an oncoming train bound for Newry, Co. Down. Eighty-eight people died, with hundreds of others being injured. Another more recent train crash was the Buttevant disaster in August 1980, when a Dublin to Cork train was derailed at high speed, killing eighteen people.

Thankfully, Ireland has had few air crashes, although the most famous is surely the Aer Lingus Flight 712 that left Cork for London on 24 March 1968. It inexplicably crashed into the sea off Tuskar Rock in Co. Wexford after departure, causing all sixty-one passengers and crew on board to lose their lives. The exact reason for the crash remains a mystery, and the cause of much speculation, including that it may have been shot down accidentally. Another heart-breaking disaster occurred at Whiddy Island, Co. Cork, when a French ship named *Betelgeuse*, carrying a full cargo of crude oil, experienced problems and arrived into the bay to carry out repairs. On 8 January 1978, the ship was consumed with flames and the highly flammable cargo exploded. The resulting fireball killed fifty people, some on the ship, others nearby on land.

Thankfully, Ireland's safety standards are among the best in the world and disasters of this type are exceptionally rare in modern times. They do still occur occasionally, however. The most prominent recent example was the explosion in the village of Creeslough, Co. Donegal, on 7 October 2022. The origin of this explosion – which took place near a petrol station in the village – is still to be determined but it destroyed several buildings nearby, including the petrol station, which was busy at the time. Ten people were killed.

6

Remarkable and Strange Irish People

Explorers and Adventurers

Ireland has produced many remarkable people throughout its history, some of whom were little known in their lifetimes. Tom Crean is today lauded in his home country due to his exploits, but it is only in recent years that his amazing deeds have been rediscovered and celebrated. Born in Co. Kerry in 1877, Crean ran away from home as a teenager, enlisting in the British Navy. He joined Robert Scott on an Antarctic expedition lasting three years in 1901 and was asked by Scott to rejoin him in 1911 in his effort to become the first leader of a party to reach the South Pole. After trekking for hundreds of miles, supplies began to run low and Scott told several of the team, including Tom Crean, to return to base. Scott and four other men persevered, reaching the South Pole but dying on the return journey, while Crean showed outstanding bravery in leading the rest of the men to safety. In 1920, with the War of Independence raging, Crean returned to Co. Kerry, where he rarely talked about his exploits – at the time in Ireland, stories of service in the British Navy were not always well received. Crean died with little fanfare in 1938 but a statue was erected to him in his home village of Annascaul in 2003.

Despite Ireland's temperate climate, it has surprisingly produced several other famous cold-weather explorers. Ernest Shackleton made several expeditions to the polar regions. In 1909, he came within 100 miles of the South Pole, the closest effort to date. His dreams of becoming the first man to set foot there were crushed in 1911 when Roald Amundsen did just that. Undeterred, Shackleton continued exploring the Antarctic region, although the Kildare man died on his fourth expedition in 1921. Several decades before, Co. Down man Francis Crozier embarked on no fewer than six early polar expeditions, although he died alongside over 100 crewmates when attempting to discover the Northwest Passage, a route to connect the Atlantic and Pacific Oceans north of Canada, in 1848. Today, Crozier gives his name to many places in the Arctic, including Crozier Island.

Robert O'Hara Burke was another Irish explorer with amazing achievements to his name. Born into a landowning family at Issercleran House, near Loughrea, Co. Galway, in 1821, Robert was an adventurous young man who enlisted in the Austrian Army before emigrating to Australia. Once there, he became a respected policeman but in 1860, the Victorian government sponsored an expedition to cross the Australian continent from south to north, believing that vast gold deposits awaited discovery. Burke applied to lead the expedition, hoping to be the first European to chart such a route. Despite having little experience in the Australian bush, he led an initially large group to success, coming within a few miles of the northern coast in February 1861 after a gruelling 1,500-mile journey. By this point, only Burke and three others remained. The party became disoriented and ran out of food on the return journey, with Burke dying on 30 June 1861. His body was found after an extensive search, and the Irishman was honoured with a state funeral in Australia. To this day, a statue stands in Melbourne to Burke and his comrade, William Wills.

Explorers have visited Ireland over the centuries as well. Christopher Columbus arrived at Galway in 1477 during one of his many expeditions and some sources claim that a Galway man named William Harris accompanied him when he discovered the Americas in 1492.

Irish Aviators

Mary Heath was another Irish adventurer with incredible achievements. She was a motorcyclist dispatch rider in the First World War and in 1917 she went to the front line in France. The Limerick native was also a superb athlete who represented Britain in the 1923 Women's Olympiad. Heath had an adventurous spirit and grew fascinated with aviation during the First World War. She took flying lessons in the mid-1920s and became the first woman in Britain to get a commercial licence. Mary was also the first woman ever to make a parachute jump from an aeroplane and was the first person to fly solo across Africa. She had many other impressive achievements and by the late 1920s she was well known throughout Ireland and beyond, including for surviving a 100mph plane crash into the concrete roof of a factory. Her achievements are all the more remarkable in light of the fact that, when she was a baby, Mary's mother had been murdered by her father, who had afterwards been committed to a mental asylum. Nevertheless, raised by her aunts, she excelled in several fields and is remembered as a remarkable pioneer of aviation to this day. She was not the only female aviator to make her mark on Ireland. Lillian Bland, who lived in Co. Antrim, flew Ireland's first powered biplane and also became the first woman in the world to design and fly her own aeroplane.

Ireland was certainly at the centre of the early decades of aviation. The landing of aviators Alcock and Brown at a rural bog outside Clifden in Co. Galway in 1919 crowned them as the first men to fly across the Atlantic Ocean after several unsuccessful attempts by others. Amazingly, they landed less than a mile from another historic landmark, the Marconi Telegraph Station, which had been established in 1907. Since then, it had transmitted messages across the Atlantic Ocean to Glace Bay, Canada, linking Europe and North America and relaying significant news, including the sinking of *Titanic* in 1912. Alcock and Brown's story of battling with freezing fog, technical issues and flying almost upside down in inclement weather was also transmitted from the station and made international headlines. Reporters from all over the world descended on the rural site to meet the flying pioneers, whose names were to enter aviation history. Another of the world's most famous pilots, Amelia Earhart, had a similar experience in 1932 when she departed Newfoundland in Canada in an attempt to become the first woman to fly solo across the Atlantic. This she did, but her plans to land in Paris were scuppered by bad weather and technical issues, so she instead landed in a field belonging to the Gallagher family in Co. Derry. A farm worker rushed to the plane, still a rare sight in those days, and enquired about where the pilot had come from. 'America,' answered Earhart.

Some decades later, another Irishman had a profound effect on aviation. The engineer James Martin of Co. Down experienced a colleague dying in a plane crash and afterwards successfully designed the ejector seat, something that has saved thousands of lives since.

Engineers, Scientists and Inventors

Ireland has had its share of inventors and engineers, too. The first female engineering graduate in the world, Alice Perry, is believed to have come from the University of Galway in 1906. The Irish are often said to have built America, and the White House itself was designed by the Kilkenny-born architect James Hoban. The first underwater vessel accepted by the US navy was invented by Clare man John Philip Holland, now considered the father of the modern submarine. Kay McNulty, a native of the Donegal Gaeltacht, moved to America without a word of English, but eventually graduated from university as a top mathematician. She was headhunted for a secret government programme to build a computer, and today Kay is rightly recognised as one of the mothers of modern-day computer programming. Arguably the father of the same discipline was the first professor of mathematics at Queen's College, Cork, George Boole. Louis Brennan was another Irish inventor extraordinaire. The Mayo watchmaker invented both the monorail and the torpedo.

There have also been many scientific advances made by the Irish. Robert Mallet, an Irish geophysicist, is often called the 'father of seismology' for his pioneering work on earthquakes. His namesake, seventeenth-century scientist Robert Boyle, is credited as the father of modern chemistry while, in 1806, Francis Beaufort, a native of Co. Meath, gave his name to the Beaufort scale, used to measure wind speed. Ireland also has a Nobel winner in the sciences. Ernest Walton, a native of Waterford, became the first person to smash the atom, ushering in the nuclear age. This led to him being honoured with the Nobel Prize in Physics in 1951.

In terms of medical advancements, the first smallpox vaccine was given to children in Dublin in 1725. The disease had devastated Ireland, some statistics indicating that it may have been responsible for one in five deaths in Dublin City at the time, with an even higher fatality rate among children. It left many others blind or disfigured. After a vaccine was developed, it was first used on several prisoners and next on five Dublin children, who received it in 1725. Two of these children died but Edward

Jenner made a further breakthrough, realising that vaccinating people with the much milder cowpox gave people immunity. By the first decades of the nineteenth century, most wealthy Irish people were receiving the vaccine against smallpox, although it would take longer for it to become more generally available. Although the disease reappeared with a vengeance during the Famine, killing thousands, smallpox would become less and less deadly as vaccination rates grew, and by the turn of the twentieth century it was largely eradicated in Ireland.

Statesmen and Politicians

Many politicians of high renown internationally were Irish or of Irish descent. Some, such as John F. Kennedy, are well known. Kennedy visited his ancestral homeland in June 1963 and was greeted with enormous cheering crowds wherever he went. He would be assassinated within months. Shortly after his passing, Kennedy's father sent a telegram to Taoiseach Éamon de Valera, stating that, 'One of the happiest and most memorable events in our son's life was his visit to Ireland in 1963.' Although many other American presidents with Irish ancestry have since visited Ireland, including Richard Nixon, Ronald Reagan, Bill Clinton, Barack Obama and Joe Biden, it is hard to find one held in the same regard as Kennedy, although Obama does have a motorway plaza named in his honour in Co. Tipperary!

Ulysses S. Grant, who became the first American president to set foot on Irish soil.

Many earlier presidents also had Irish ancestry and no fewer than seven of the first American presidents had strong family links with Co. Antrim. Before Kennedy, these presidents were invariably of Northern Protestant stock and often labelled their ancestry as 'Scotch-Irish' or 'Ulster Scots'. These include Andrew Jackson, Harry Truman, Grover Cleveland, Andrew Johnson and Ulysses S. Grant, the latter being the first president to set foot on Irish soil, although this was after his tenure in office.

The names of some Irish politicians who made high office elsewhere are less recognisable in their home country. Daniel Pollen of Dublin and John Ballance of Antrim both rose to the office of Prime Minister of New Zealand. William Penn, the founder of the state of Pennsylvania, spent much of his youth in Ireland. Chaim Herzog, a president of the state of Israel, was born in Belfast, although he spent his childhood in Dublin where his father was chief Rabbi of Ireland. Napoleon was not of Irish descent but had many Irish connections nonetheless. His horse was likely to have been bred in Ireland, while his life was also saved by an Irish priest when he fell into a river while out hunting. His surgeon, Dr Barry O'Meara, was Irish, while 'The Little Corporal' also met Wolfe Tone.

Napoleon's fellow countryman, Charles de Gaulle, did have Irish ancestry. His forebear, Patrick McCartan, was hanged and subsequently beheaded as a rebel by the British at Carrickfergus in 1653. De Gaulle often spoke of his interest in learning more about this ancestry. Not everyone was so proud of their Irish roots, however. Arthur Wellesley, the first Duke of Wellington, who went on to be the British Prime Minister on two occasions, was from a large land-owning Anglo-Irish family and served as an MP for Trim, Co. Meath, for several years. He did not advertise this fact and is reported to have said, when his Irish lineage was mentioned, that, 'To be born in a stable does not make one a horse,' although this is a quotation that some historians dispute.

The Lesser-Known Irish Diaspora

Unsurprisingly, the Irish diaspora is enormous and the American census of 2020 indicated that there were close to 40 million citizens of that country claiming Irish descent. The first immigrant through the gates of Ellis Island, New York, was Cork teenager Annie Moore, just 15 years of age when she disembarked in 1892. Consequently, there are far more people of Irish ancestry outside of Ireland than within it. The largest St Patrick's Day Parade does not even take place in Ireland. In fact, New York's parade, which can attract up to 2 million spectators, is the world's oldest and largest celebration. The inaugural parade took place all the way back on 17 March 1762, fourteen years prior to the signing of the American Declaration of Independence, and it continues to be held annually to this day.

It is well known that Irish immigrants have made huge contributions to the United States, Canada, Australia, New Zealand and Britain. Perhaps less remembered is the influx of Irishmen and women into South America. Early settlers Juan and Tomas Farrell helped to found Argentina's capital, Buenos Aries, in the sixteenth century. The majority of the Irish people destined for South America, upwards of 40,000 settlers, mostly from the midlands and south-east, arrived to the continent in the nineteenth century, however. The Irish language was spoken among some immigrants for a generation in South America and there remain long-established hurling clubs in Argentina. In the same country, up to half a million people today claim some Irish ancestry. Mayo native William Brown earned the title of 'Father of the Argentine Navy' and played a pivotal role in the country's fight for independence. Singer Chris de Burgh was born in Argentina and Eamon Bulfin, who fought in the Easter Rising, was also among those of Irish descent born there. Che Guevara, an Argentinian native and fighter in the Cuban Revolution, also had strong links with the Lynches of Galway, members of the family having emigrated to Argentina in the eighteenth century, and he spoke openly about his pride in his Irish heritage. Argentina was not the only South American country to receive Irish immigrants. Bernardo O'Higgins Riquelme, born in 1778, was unsurprisingly of Irish ancestry, as his name may suggest, and he was an important leader in the war for Chilean independence from Spanish rule.

The Irish also went to the Caribbean in relatively large numbers. Montserrat in particular is home to a large proportion of people who claim Irish descent, with surnames such as O'Donoghue, Farrell and Daley remaining common on the island. This wave of immigration mainly dates to the seventeenth century, many being forced from Ireland in Cromwellian times as indentured servants. The accent on the island resembles the Irish accent to this day and towns such as Kinsale, Cork Hill and St Patrick's hint at the strong Irish connection on 'the Emerald Isle of The Caribbean'. It is the only country in the world other than Ireland to mark St Patrick's Day as a national holiday, although Nigeria considers St Patrick among its patron saints as well. South Africa also has its own Irish diaspora. Some went there during the various gold and diamond rushes, while others stayed after fighting on either side of the Second Boer War. Major John MacBride was one prominent Irishman who fought for the Boers in their struggle. He was later executed for his role in the Easter Rising.

The Oldest People in Irish History

Officially, the title of the oldest person in Irish history belongs to Kathleen Snavely, born Kathleen Hayes, in Co. Clare in 1901. She passed away in the United States in 2015 at the age of 113.

However, in earlier times, when age verification was far more difficult, many individuals were said to have reached even greater ages. One of the most legendary claims is that of Katherine Fitzgerald, the Countess of Desmond, from Inchiquin Castle in Co. Cork. She was reputed to have died at 140 years old after falling from a cherry tree. Sir Walter Raleigh even recounted her story in his writings. Though such an age seems implausible, it is hard to disprove, especially considering birth certificates were not commonly issued before the mid-nineteenth century. Many elderly people did not know their precise age, making it tricky to establish historical longevity with certainty.

An 1860 edition of the *Tuam Herald* newspaper noted remarkable lifespans in the west of Ireland, however. It referenced a man named John Palace of Kilmeena, said to have died in 1857 at 115. His hearing was said to be so sharp that he could herd cattle away from crops despite being nearly blind. Margaret Walsh of Ballinrobe was another notable centenarian, reportedly aged 112 at the time. In 1898, various international newspapers reported on Anne Armstrong of Spanish Point, Co. Clare, who was said to be 116 and the world's oldest living woman at the time. She lived alone in a cottage, supported by caring neighbours.

The 1901 Irish census recorded many super-centenarians. Among them were James Keating, 115, from Belfast, and Cornelius Doherty, 116, from Donegal but the oldest listed was John McDonagh of Clifden, Co. Galway, recorded as 122 years old. He died in September 1901, shortly after the census was conducted, though some newspapers then claimed he was 125, backed by testimony from local priests. A native Irish speaker, McDonagh recalled the 1798 landing of French forces under General Humbert and had helped build Slyne Head lighthouse at the age of 60. His second wife, Anne King, outlived him and was still lively at 78 years. By the 1911 census, the oldest residents were Patrick Reynolds (113) of Co. Roscommon, and John Connolly (114) of Co. Laois. In the early years of the Irish Free

State, several super-centenarians were also reported. One was Neal Boyce of Co. Donegal, who died in 1927, allegedly aged 115. His diet reportedly consisted solely of potatoes, oat porridge and oat bread, and he had never ventured more than 15 miles from home. In 1934, John Joyce of Leenane, Co. Galway, was said to have passed away at 117.

Among the most beloved Irish centenarians was Bridget Dirrane, who lived to 109 and led a remarkable life. Born on the Aran Islands in 1894, she met revolutionaries like Patrick Pearse and Thomas MacDonagh in her youth and joined Cumann na mBan, a revolutionary group for Irish women. Imprisoned in Mountjoy during the struggle for independence, she went on hunger strike, spoke Irish to her guards, and danced jigs in defiance. After independence, she emigrated to America, worked as a nurse and in a munitions factory during the Second World War, campaigned for John F. Kennedy, and married two brothers named Dirrane. Later in life, she returned to Inishmore, remained a vibrant community figure, and published her memoir, *Woman of Aran*, in 2003, the year she passed away. Her advice for long life? 'I do not like to preach, but try a little kindness. Think positively and act swiftly. And to the young people: stick to your books, avail of the educational opportunities available to you, and eat green vegetables.'[13]

Ireland continues to celebrate those who reach a great age and Irish centenarians still receive a personal letter and a gift from the president each year after turning 100.

---

13 Dirrane, B., *A Woman of Aran* (2003), p.79.

Irish Giants

Ireland has also been home to many people of exceptional height throughout the centuries, with perhaps the most famous being Charles Byrne, nicknamed simply 'the Irish Giant'. Born in Co. Derry in 1762, Byrne reportedly stood at an astonishing height of at least 7ft 6in, a remarkable figure even today, let alone in the eighteenth century when the average male height was approximately 5ft 6in. Some contemporary reports even claimed Byrne surpassed 8ft. Both of his parents were of average stature and Byrne's extraordinary growth was believed to have been caused by a tumour on his pituitary gland. Seeking opportunity, the Derry man moved to England, where he toured the country as part of public exhibitions. Audiences flocked to see the gentle giant, drawn both by his incredible stature and his kind nature. He earned a significant sum of money, which he always carried on his person. Tragically, while in a public house, he was robbed of his entire savings, around £700. Devastated, he fell into a deep depression and turned to heavy drinking. Already in poor health due to his condition, Byrne died at just 22 years old. His final wish was for a burial at sea beneath 20 fathoms of water so that his body could not be dissected. Newspapers initially reported that local fishermen in Margate had honoured this request. However, just days later, it was revealed that famed anatomist John Hunter had paid £500 for Byrne's body, which was duly dissected. His skeleton was displayed at the Hunterian Museum in London for over 200 years. After years of campaigning to respect Byrne's final wishes, his remains were finally removed from public display in 2023.

Among other notably tall Irishmen were the Knipe brothers, also from Co. Derry, identical twins who toured in the 1780s as the 'Gigantic Irish Twins'. Some reports stated that they were cousins of Charles Byrne. Both standing at 7ft 2in, their height was exaggerated as being closer to 8ft by showmen. One theatrical advertisement claimed, 'The sight of them is more than the mind can conceive, the tongue express, or pencil delineate … we scarce shall look upon their like again.' Another towering figure was Patrick Cotter of Co. Cork, born around 1760. Cotter toured England as a spectacle after he was allegedly sold by his father to a showman as a teenager. Initially underpaid and poorly treated, Cotter was at one point imprisoned for refusing to perform until better compensated. Eventually, he gained more control over his career, adopting the stage name Patrick O'Brien and claiming descent from Brian Boru. He later earned up to £10 a day and lived a relatively long life for someone of his stature, dying aged 46 in 1806. Wary of posthumous exploitation, Cotter had his body buried in three coffins, under concrete, and behind iron bars in a Bristol chapel. A century later, during drainage works, his skeleton was rediscovered and officially measured – he stood just shy of 8ft tall.

Ireland's fascination with extraordinary height did not fade with time. In 1987, an episode of *The Late Late Show* showcased three Irishmen, each around 6ft 9in tall, and invited viewers to nominate anyone they knew to be taller! On the opposite end of the spectrum, the shortest Irishman is believed to have been David Jones of Lisburn, Co. Antrim. Newspaper reports from March 1970 suggest he was around 2ft 2in tall at the time of his death, though he may have been slightly taller. Jones lived to be 68 and was a beloved figure in his community, known for delivering firewood with his horse and cart.

Other Remarkable Irish People

Two other remarkable women of Irish history were the Ladies of Llangollen, described shortly after their deaths as:

> Lady Eleanor Butler and Miss Ponsonby, Irish ladies of rank and beauty, who loved each other with an affection so true that they could never bear the idea of the separation which the marriage of either would necessitate. They, therefore, resolved on lives of celibacy, and, refusing many handsome offers, fled from home.[14]

The pair, both from wealthy aristocratic backgrounds, fell in love and fled Kilkenny in 1778, when Sarah was 23 and Eleanor 39, setting up home in North Wales and leaving their privileged lives behind them. They lived together in the village of Llangollen for some fifty years, with Eleanor's diary describing in detail a harmonious homelife where she describes Sarah as 'My Beloved'. The women's unconventional life for the time, although invariably described as celibate, captured the public imagination and they received many distinguished visitors, among them the Duke of Wellington and William Wordsworth. They grew well known and prints of the women during their lifetime can be found in the British Museum.

Mary Mallon, a cook from Co. Tyrone, also gained international notoriety that led to her being given the unflattering moniker 'Typhoid Mary'. Born in 1869, Mallon emigrated to the United States aged 15. After settling in New York, she worked as a domestic servant and, with her hard-working nature and talent for cooking, she was soon employed as a personal chef for a succession of upper-class families. Unfortunately for Mary, typhoid was rampant in New York at the time and, despite not becoming sick with the disease, she unknowingly carried and spread it. Between 1900 and 1907, she worked in the homes of no fewer than seven families and, in each one, people grew ill or died. It was not until she took a position as a cook for an upper-class family on Long Island that it was discovered she was a healthy

---

14 Prichard, J., *An Account of the Ladies of Llangollen* (1923), p.2.

carrier of the bacteria. She was therefore believed to be at the heart of a typhoid fever outbreak in New York, earning her the unflattering title of 'the most dangerous woman in America'. In 1907, with authorities increasingly desperate to contain the disease, Mary was exiled to an isolation facility outside New York, where she was placed in solitary confinement so she could not infect others. Having committed no crime, Mary hired a lawyer to protest her incarceration and she was released but warned not to resume employment as a cook. She did not obey this directive, returning to working in kitchens under an assumed name. Several other people died of typhoid in these houses too, and when authorities tracked her down in 1915, she was put in isolation again, this time for good. She died twenty-three years later, still in captivity.

Another remarkable Irish native who gained fame in America was James O'Connell. He appeared in the 1840s to large crowds as part of P.T. Barnum's famed circus. He was exhibited as 'the World's First Tattooed Showman'. Dublin-born O'Connell explained some of his back story to the crowds, who paid 25 cents for the privilege. He had been shipwrecked on a Pacific Island called Pohnpei, now part of Micronesia, and danced a jig to please the native islanders, who he said had considered killing and eating him. He had earned their trust and lived among them, getting tattooed from head to toe before being rescued and embarking on his nationwide tour. O'Connell's story resonated with America and he struck gold when he partnered with Barnum, the world's greatest promoter.

Cork woman Nellie Cashman also struck gold. After emigrating to the United States, she made her way to gold rush boomtowns in Nevada, the Klondike and Alaska, occasionally mining herself but also setting up a successful business to serve the miners' needs. In the winter of 1874, Nellie was in Victoria, Canada, when she heard of an outbreak of scurvy and a severe shortage of food at the mining site in remote Cassiar. She gathered a party that collected as much food and relief items as they could and then trudged through the snow for seventy-seven days to reach the miners. She became known as the 'Angel of the Cassiar' for this act, which probably saved many lives. She also later became the first woman to cast a vote in an Alaskan election and a philanthropist that helped to set up a hospital in Victoria.

One of the richest men in world history, John William Mackay, was also a beneficiary of a gold rush. A native of Dublin, Mackay emigrated from Ireland as a desperately poor man in 1840. Initially a miner in California, MacKay made enough money to fund the opening of his own mines, including the Bonanza Mine in the Sierra Nevada mountains. This produced over $100 million worth of gold and silver. Despite his enormous wealth, MacKay continued to work hard, often digging out mines himself alongside his workers. He later used his huge fortune to branch into transatlantic cabling, leading to the laying of a cable across the Atlantic Ocean from America to Co. Kerry. MacKay died in 1902, worth an estimated $1 billion, the equivalent of close to $80 billion today.

Ireland even had its own short-lived gold rush in 1795. An accidental discovery of the precious metal at Ballinvalley near Avoca, Co. Wicklow, led to a huge influx of miners desperate to uncover more. About 80kg of gold was extracted in the first few weeks but, predictably enough, the government forced prospectors off the land. Over the next few years, thousands more ounces of gold would be discovered intermittently in the area but the mother lode, if it exists, has yet to be uncovered. Ireland also had one discovery of a gem-quality diamond. This occurred in 1816 when a young girl found an uncut diamond lying in the Colebrook River in Co. Fermanagh. It was given to Lady Brookeborough, a member of the local gentry, and came to be known as the Brookeborough Diamond.

There have been some remarkable Irish animals also. The oldest cow in the world called Ireland home, for example. Big Bertha lived on the O'Leary farm in Sneem, Co. Kerry, dying aged 48 years old on New Year's Eve, 1993, having given birth to an astonishing thirty-nine calves. Towards the end of her life, she was a regular at fairs and became something of a local celebrity. Bertha was given a wake after her death and she even has a local gin named in her honour. The oldest recorded wild bird in the world, a Manx Shearwater, was recorded in the Copeland Islands off Co. Down, having reached a scarcely believable 55 years of age. Paddy the Pigeon was another famous Irish animal. The homing pigeon had been hatched and raised in Co. Antrim and was awarded the PDSA Dickin Medal in September 1944, after flying coded information from Normandy to Britain during the D-Day landings. He helped turn the tide of the Second World War and is honoured with a plaque in his home village of Carnlough.

Ireland is synonymous with horse racing and some of the best horses in the world were bred and born here. These include Co. Kilkenny's Red Rum, a horse that would go on to dominate the sport in the 1970s, winning no fewer than three Grand Nationals at Aintree. Istabraq was another incredible racehorse that won three consecutive champion hurdles at Cheltenham. Shergar was a third Irish horse who was worth millions after cruising to victory in the 1981 Epsom Derby. The colt was kidnapped from Ballymany Stud in Co. Kildare by an armed gang in February 1983. The kidnappers, who were seeking a ransom, negotiated with the syndicate that owned the horse in the days directly after the incident, but broke off all communication at an early stage. Shergar's body was never found, in what remains one of the most mysterious occurrences in Irish history, although it is believed that he was shot shortly after being kidnapped as the powerful horse panicked and the kidnappers were unable to handle him.

Greyhound racing has also long been a popular pastime in the country and Master McGrath, born the runt of a litter of seven pups in Co. Waterford, arguably grew up to be the most famous greyhound ever. Apparently, the trainer considered drowning the pup, who was small and weak, and its life was saved by the intercession of a local boy who begged for the dog to be let live. This decision was vindicated when Master McGrath, a completely unknown prospect, won the prestigious Waterloo Cup in style in 1868. He went on to win it on two more occasions, making his owner a very wealthy man. The greyhound was even paraded in front of Queen Victoria. Master McGrath died shortly after his last Waterloo Cup win in 1871. It was a sudden death with some rumours that foul play had been involved, although an autopsy showed that Master McGrath's heart was unusually large for a dog, something that may have explained his speed but also caused his early death. Another greyhound, Offaly's Mick the Miller, had a similarly storied career, breaking six world records in the 1920s and '30s, and at one stage winning nineteen high-class races in a row. It was said in his heyday that he was as popular and well known as any human sports star. *Wild Boy*, a film based on his life, starring Mick the Miller himself, was released in 1934 and a statue to the greyhound now stands in his home village of Killeigh.

7

Strange but True in Irish Sport

The Tailteann Games and Ancient Irish Sport

Ireland has played various types of sport for millennia. Its own version of the Olympics, the Tailteann Games, was inaugurated some 3,000 years ago and featured events such as the long jump, chariot racing, swimming, wrestling, boxing and spear throwing. A modern incarnation of the Tailteann Games was organised on three occasions after independence as a festival and celebration of the Irish nation. The first instance, the 1924 Games, was hugely successful and attended by some 250,000 spectators, who watched thousands of competitors taking part in dozens of events. The Games included some of the foremost athletes in the world at the time and the number of competitors even dwarfed the Paris Olympics of the same summer. Despite these early successes, the event was held for the third and last time in 1932.

Hurling, Gaelic football and handball are among the sports that owe their origins to Ireland. Hurling, the national sport of the country, has been played for thousands of years and is mentioned regularly in Irish legends. Cúchulainn, Ireland's foremost mythical warrior, was mentioned regularly as a top-class hurler who was given his name (Cú Chulainn – the hound of Cullen) after he drove a sliotar, or hurling ball, down the throat of a fierce guard dog. The dog belonged to a chieftain named Cullen and Setanta gave him his word that he would act as his guard dog from then on, earning the name. Early stories equate the game of hurling to a form of martial training, and being a good hurler was considered a prerequisite to being a brave warrior. The English disapproved of hurling and the fourteenth-century Statutes of Kilkenny namechecked the game as a peculiarly Irish pastime and warned the Anglo-Normans against playing it, lest they become more Irish than the Irish themselves. Nevertheless, it survived and hurling had several different names across the country, including iomán and scuaib, the rules of which varied considerably from place to place. This lack of a rulebook meant that it could be brutal. In 1785, one Michael Brennan was accused of murdering Patrick McDarby during a hurling game in Co. Laois after he hit him on the side of the head with his hurley.

Gaelic football's origins are difficult to pinpoint. Types of football have been played all over the world for thousands of years and a game known as 'caid' (still the Irish language word for football in Munster) was known to have been played in Co. Kerry and surrounding districts hundreds of years ago. It also existed in Leinster and whole villages took part, attempting to get a ball from one place to another. The rules were few and any means of travelling with the ball appears to have been permitted. Other mentions of football can be found from the fourteenth century onwards, but what resemblance it bore to modern Gaelic football can only be guessed at. It is likely the rules also changed drastically depending on where it was being played. Handball is also of ancient origin, with versions of the game being played all over Europe for hundreds of years, although by the nineteenth century it was played widely in Ireland, with local championships run all over the country. The game was brought by immigrants to the United States, where there remains a popular handball scene to this day.

These may have been the typical sports of the lower classes over many centuries, but in the decades after the Famine which decimated the rural population, English sports were becoming codified and gaining popularity. Cricket, soccer and rugby caught the imagination of many landlords, who patronised the games for their tenants. Cricket had become particularly popular by the mid-nineteenth century, pushing hurling into ever-smaller pockets of the country. Policeman and government officials, meanwhile, discouraged Gaelic football and hurling. The founding of the Gaelic Athletic Association in Co. Tipperary in 1884 changed everything. The GAA aimed to reinstate these traditionally Irish pastimes. Founded by seven men in a hotel in Thurles, Co. Tipperary, the GAA successfully tied itself to Irishness and clubs were regularly named after Irish heroes of old. The organisation was astonishingly successful and the ancient game of hurling retook precedence within a few years of its establishment, eventually overtaking cricket in popularity throughout the land. Gaelic football, too, grew exponentially and was shortly the most popular sport in many places in the country. Today, the All-Ireland hurling and football finals, both held each summer, attract over 82,000 spectators to Croke Park.

Other Sports in Ireland

Although the first official soccer club in Ireland, Cliftonville in Belfast, was not founded until 1879, the game had been played recreationally for decades before this. Cliftonville were forced to play a local rugby team for the first fixture, although they still managed to lose 2–1! Ireland's first international match was held in Belfast in early 1882. It resulted in a chastening 13–0 defeat to England in front of some 2,500 disgruntled home fans.

In terms of the rules of soccer, Ireland's main contribution was the penalty kick. A goalkeeper named William McCrum from Milford FC in Co. Armagh was an official of the Irish Football Association. Angered by defenders continually professionally fouling attackers who were in on goal, he suggested in 1890 that a penalty kick would be a suitably severe punishment for an infraction committed when defending near the goal. Many were against the idea of penalties, but Ireland trialled the rule and other national football associations eventually followed suit and adopted it. It remains part of the rules to this day.

Rugby gained popularity even earlier than soccer. Dublin University, founded in 1854, was the first organised Rugby Football Club on the island and is the oldest rugby club still in existence in the world. Two separate national rugby federations were founded by 1874, merging as the Irish Rugby Football Union five years later. Ireland's first international was played the following year against England. The teams had twenty players on each side and England won 'two points to nil', a scoring system having yet to be fully set down in the sport. Rugby was growing very popular and even the man who would go on to found the Gaelic Athletic Association, Michael Cusack, was an enthusiastic participant of the game.

Cricket retained strongholds after the foundation of the Gaelic Athletic Association, particularly around Dublin. In fact, the only Nobel-winning author to have played first-class cricket is Irish playwright Samuel Beckett, who played several matches for a Dublin University side against Northamptonshire in the mid-1920s. Blayney 'Bud' Hamilton, a native of Co. Louth, could be Ireland's most versatile athlete ever, representing the country in cricket but also in badminton, hockey and tennis. Tennis had something of a golden age in Ireland in the final two decades of the nineteenth century, Irish players winning no fewer than nine Wimbledon titles (four in men's singles, one in ladies' singles, two in men's doubles, and two in mixed doubles). Irish players also won several important tennis opens and two Olympic gold medals under the flag of the United Kingdom. Blayney Hamilton's brother, Willoughby, was one of the foremost stars, being the world No. 1-ranked player for several years, triumphing in Wimbledon in 1890, while Lena Rice from Co. Tipperary completed a famous double in the same year by winning the women's singles. Incredibly, Ireland also won the doubles competition that year – Frank Stoker, an international rugby player and cousin of *Dracula* writer Bram Stoker, was one member of the triumphant pair. These incredible successes must have seemed to auger well for the future of Irish tennis, but Harold Mahony's 1896 win was the last time Ireland would experience victory at Wimbledon.

Unlikely Irish Sporting Connections

There are many sports internationally that owe some of their growth or popularity to Irish people, including several sports that would not be traditionally associated with the country. Irish-Americans played a huge role in early baseball, for example. The parents of Roger Connor, the sport's all-time home-run leader before Babe Ruth, had arrived in America just five years before his birth from the town of Tralee, Co. Kerry. Connor was proud of his roots, regularly wearing a shamrock on his jersey. Connor also visited Tralee in the 1920s, after he had retired from the game, and called to relatives in the land of his parents' birth. When asked by a cousin for an address to allow him to stay in touch, the well-known baseballer replied 'Roger Conner, America, will reach me!' Both of the first two major league players to win 300 games were also Irish-American, namely Pud Galvin and Tim Keefe. Patsy Donovan is also largely unknown in Ireland but played a major role in baseball after he and his family escaped post-Famine Ireland in the late 1850s. The Donovans settled in Massachusetts and Patsy picked up 'America's game' as a young boy. His career would take him to teams in several states before he went on to become one of the sport's most decorated managers. Donovan went on to coach none other than future American president George Bush Snr.

The games of Australian Rules football and Gaelic football certainly also have a common ancestor, one theory being that when post-famine emigrants from Ireland to Victoria in Australia played 'caid', other nationalities quickly joined in the fun, leading to the codification of Australian Rules football at the tail end of the 1850s, over two decades before Gaelic football was similarly regulated. The game of shinty from Scotland also certainly has similar origins to hurling. Even ice hockey is believed to owe some of its origins to this ancient Irish game, many of its earliest players being of Irish descent, although field hockey must surely get a look in in this case too.

The 'Father of British Polo' is also an Irishman. John Henry Watson, born in Ballydarton in Co. Carlow in 1851, was an avid hunter and horseman and he began organising polo matches in the 1870s. These proved popular among the upper classes and the All-Ireland Polo Club was founded shortly afterwards. Watson went on to help draft the rules for the game, which had yet to be properly codified, and to be part of the first team to win the international cup in polo in 1876. Such was his enthusiasm for polo, Watson suffered a heart attack during a match in Phoenix Park in 1905. He died in 1908, but will be remembered as a hugely influential figure in the game. Interestingly, the Watson family must have been hunters for generations, as it is believed that the last wolf to be killed in Ireland was shot in 1786 by a farmer named John Watson, of Ballydarton, Co. Carlow, whose sheep were being attacked. He was a direct ancestor of John Henry Watson.

Another interesting sporting connection in Ireland was the first-ever captain of the indomitable New Zealand rugby team, Dave Gallaher. He and his family emigrated to New Zealand from Donegal in around 1878, settling on the North Island. Dave grew to 6ft and was a talented sportsman, joining a rugby club near Auckland where he was found to be a forward of some ability. He was quickly called up to the national squad and was chosen by teammates as captain for the 1905 tour of Europe and North America, the country's rugby team's first foray outside of Oceania. They wore a strip of black jerseys, black shorts and black socks, which led to them being nicknamed the All-Blacks, a nickname that has stuck to this day. Gallaher played against his home country in November 1905, the Kiwis triumphing 15–0. It proved to be a hugely successful tour and New Zealand lost just one match, to Wales. Gallaher would go on to play thirty-six matches for New Zealand and co-write the classic rugby manual *The Complete Rugby Footballer*. He died in action in the First World War in 1917 but is still remembered fondly, both in his native land and in his adopted home.

Unusual Events in Irish Sport

Boxing was a hugely popular spectator sport in the nineteenth century and Ireland produced many world-famous boxers with interesting back stories. Dan Donnelly was one such character. Born in Dublin in 1788, by adulthood he was standing at over 6ft. Donnelly was a good sportsman in several disciplines but was attracted to the sport of bare-knuckle boxing, which was growing in popularity. At this time, English fighters regularly toured Ireland, and a local army captain noticed Donnelly's strength and power and encouraged him to challenge one of them. Donnelly agreed and, after several months' training, he faced off against renowned English fighter Tom Hall on 14 September 1814 in front of some 40,000 people at Belcher's Hollow, near the Curragh in Co. Kildare. The fight ended in a controversial draw, many feeling that the Irishman had been cheated, but Donnelly was undeterred. He next challenged and beat an even more formidable English boxer, George Cooper, and became a national hero in the process.

A third bout against Englishman Tom Oliver lasted thirty-two rounds and again saw Donnelly emerge triumphant. Donnelly was charming and well liked in his home country, although he had a fondness for alcohol. He died after a short illness, barely a year after the Oliver fight in 1820, his funeral drawing a huge crowd to Dublin. A memorial now stands to Donnelly at the site of his first fight, now renamed Donnelly's Hollow in his honour. Gruesomely, a mummified arm said to have been severed from Donnelly's body was on display in the Hideout Public House in Kildare until 1953. An equally famous boxer at the time was Dubliner Jack Langan, who fought for the first time aged 13. He was Irish champion by 1819, afterwards travelling to South America to fight with Simon Bolívar for the independence of the nations there. He later spent some time in prison before losing a seventy-seven-round bout against English champion Tom Spring.

Ireland was also a place where travelling boxers knew they could attract a good crowd. The African-American fighter Tom Molineux was one of the most famous boxers in the nineteenth century and fate saw that he died, and was buried, in the west of Ireland. Born into slavery in Virginia in 1784, Molineux impressed crowds in his native country with his strength and technique. He was considered a fine boxer in America but, at that time, boxers had to make their mark in Europe to be considered the best in the world. As a result, Molineux sailed to England in 1809 and, after a string of high-profile victories, he challenged English champion Tom Cribb in what was considered a world title fight. The match took place in 1810 and, after a gruelling contest lasting thirty-three rounds, Molineux lost under highly controversial circumstances. He continued to box until 1815, before taking up touring. Molineux toured Ireland in 1817, and by the summer of 1818 he found himself in Galway. It was here that he was discovered sick and destitute on the streets, possibly suffering from both alcohol addiction and tuberculosis. He was taken in by the army but died on 4 August, aged just 34. Molineux was buried in an unmarked grave. A headstone was finally erected there in 2019, a century on, to honour a man who had risen from slavery to become one of the most prominent athletes in the world.

Irish Sporting Scandals

All Irish sports have had their fair share of bizarre, strange and shocking moments, but Irish soccer was the only one torn apart with partition on the horizon. Many in the south felt that the IFA, headquartered in Belfast, already had a bias in favour of northern and unionist players, and the conflict over the War of Independence in 1921 led to a schism. To this day, Northern Ireland and the Republic of Ireland field two separate teams in soccer, even though sports such as rugby, hockey and cricket all manage to play successfully under the All-Ireland banner. Confusingly, the sport in the north is run by the Irish Football Association (IFA) while in the republic it is organised by the similarly named Football Association of Ireland (FAI). This split also led to the foundation of separate club leagues in the north and south. The league in the north has often seen sectarian tensions. One truly shocking story was that of the disbandment of Belfast Celtic, a traditionally Catholic club, in 1949. Founded in 1891, Belfast Celtic had found themselves in Northern Ireland after partition. The Northern Irish League was dominated by unionist clubs but Celtic played on and were successful, winning the competition fourteen times. They were twice forced to withdraw from the competition, however, with violence among supporters marring many of their games. On St Stephen's Day, 1948, Celtic squared up against their deadly rivals Linfield FC, a bastion of loyalism. The game finished in a 1–1 draw, but Linfield supporters rushed the field at the final whistle, attacking several players from the Celtic side. Jimmy Jones, a centre forward, was particularly badly injured, being thrown over a parapet and ending up unconscious with a broken leg. Belfast Celtic disbanded shortly afterwards.

Violence such as this leaves other sporting scandals in the ha'penny place, although even mentioning the name of the island of Saipan will bring to many people's mind the scandal that gripped Ireland in 2002. A highly regarded Irish soccer team had qualified for the Japan–South Korea World Cup in that year and, led by the talented captain Roy Keane and experienced manager Mick McCarthy, many believed that they could exceed their wonderful achievements of 1990 when they had reached the World Cup quarter-finals in Italy. Unfortunately, there were pre-existing tensions between the manager and captain. These escalated during a training camp on Saipan Island, with Keane publicly criticising the team's preparations, including what he viewed as poor facilities and management. He was also accused of using unflattering language to describe the management team. After a heated argument, Keane was sent back home to Ireland just over a week before the team were to play Cameroon in their first match. Keane's absence was a significant blow to Ireland's chances and the Taoiseach of the day, Bertie Ahern, even offered to mediate, to no avail. The debate polarised Ireland, many believing that Keane should have represented his country regardless of circumstances, others sharing his criticism of the FAI and their poor planning for the tournament. Either way, the controversy overshadowed Ireland's World Cup campaign, which ended in a narrow defeat to Spain in the second round, leaving many to wonder what Ireland might have achieved had their most influential player been on the pitch.

The GAA has also had its fair share of unusual incidents and controversies. Foremost among them was the organisation's controversial decision to remove the president of Ireland, Douglas Hyde, as a patron in 1938 after he attended a soccer match in contravention of the GAA's ban on members supporting foreign sports, a ban that remained in place until 1971. The fact that he was acting as a head of state did not change minds at the time, although the GAA stadium in Hyde's home county of Roscommon was named Dr Hyde Park in the 1960s, perhaps indicating awareness of the wrong that had been done to him.

In earlier years, the GAA was not as well organised as it would come to be. The 1899 Munster football final, a game that was actually played in 1900, was a good example. This match between Tipperary and Cork was abandoned at half-time due to a burst ball and no replacement being available. Tipperary had been well ahead at half-time and they only agreed to play one half in the reply, demanding that their scores be added for both halves over the two different games, something that would have led to them being victorious. The GAA would not assent to this and Tipperary were thrown out of the competition after refusing to return to the field of play after half-time!

Six years earlier, the All-Ireland football final had been abandoned due to a pitch invasion and injuries to players, leading to Cork refusing to return to the pitch and Wexford being awarded the title. The 1903 football final, actually played in July 1905, was also mired in controversy. As the game drew to close, a Kerry player took a shot that missed the target. It went wide but hit a supporter and rebounded back onto the field. The referee did not notice and the ball was duly kicked to the net by a Kerry forward. The goal was allowed, much to Kildare's fury, whose supporters invaded the pitch and the game was abandoned. A replay was duly ordered, although also Kildare lost this!

Another unusual GAA moment was the 1939 All-Ireland final. Played on 3 September, the day that the Second World War was declared, there was a reasonable expectation of good weather for the time of year. It was not to be and torrential rain was said to have caused the dye from the players' jerseys to run into their togs. Incredibly, the second half opened with a terrific thunderstorm and flashes of lightning illuminating the Croke Park arena as supporters ran for cover. It has since been named the 'thunder and lightning final', as play continued. Incidentally Kilkenny, the maestros of hurling, won the day on a scoreline of 2–7 to 3–3, despite a Cork goal scored by the future Taoiseach, Jack Lynch.

A few years afterwards, an All-Ireland football final was played abroad, in the Polo Grounds, New York. It took place in 1947, 100 years after the Great Famine's most devastating year.

The Polo Grounds, New York, which played host to the 1947 All-Ireland football final. (Library of Congress)

Cavan played Kerry in the sweltering heat in a unique match that was broadcast by radio across the Atlantic Ocean. The American broadcast line had only been booked until 5 p.m. on the day, however, and the game was delayed starting. As the game neared its conclusion, commentator Michael O'Hehir realised that the five o'clock deadline was looming and the broadcast could be disconnected with just minutes remaining in the tightly contested game. Thousands of listeners in Ireland could hear him continually begging on air: 'If there is someone out there, please just give us five minutes more.' O'Hehir was not sure if anyone was listening but the line stayed open, and the entire All-Ireland final was broadcast back to Ireland. Cavan won the day by four points.

The Sam Maguire Cup, which is presented to the winners of the All-Ireland football championship, made its way back to New York in 1981 when Kerry were champions. Due to appear at a ceremony, it duly went missing from a safe and could not be located for a full week. The FBI were even briefly involved and a $1,000 reward was offered. The cup eventually turned up wrapped in a black bag, although it had been defaced with the words 'Up Roscommon'.

Another bizarre story from the GAA is the supposed Mayo curse. Mayo had been a powerhouse in the All-Ireland football championship between 1936 and 1951, winning three All-Ireland titles in that time. In 1951, they overcame their rivals from Meath by five points in front of 78,000 spectators at Croke Park. This was their second All-Ireland title in a row and the future seemed bright. Mayo did not reach another All-Ireland final until 1989, however. They duly lost this decider and since that time they have lost eleven more All-Ireland football finals without a win. This unusually bad streak is put down in some quarters to a curse. Rumour has it that in 1951, as they returned from Dublin celebrating their victory, the players came across a funeral in a small Mayo village. The priest officiating at the funeral urged the players to stop the lorry immediately and sympathise with the mourners. Caught up in their celebrations, however, they did not do so, and it is said that the priest cursed them that as long as any of the players shall live, Mayo would never win another All-Ireland football title. Curses of this type are not unheard of in sport – Clare's hurlers were also said to be cursed. They soldiered on for eighty-one years without winning a title until 1995, when they were finally successful. In their case, the curse had allegedly been placed on them by a local healer named Biddy Early. However, Early had died before the GAA had even been inaugurated in 1884 and Clare had won an All-Ireland after this point in 1914, making this curse seem even more far-fetched than most!

Irish Olympians

Ireland has had many remarkable Olympians over the years. The first modern Olympic winner, James Brendan Connolly, had a strong Irish connection. His parents were from the Aran Islands. The Boston native represented America in 1896 in the Athens Olympics, winning first place in the hop, skip and jump, now known as the triple jump. Indeed, many Irish Olympians won medals for other countries, mostly Britain. Among them was Louth native, Beatrice Hill-Lowe, who became the first Irish woman to win a medal when she picked up the bronze in 1908 for archery. But other countries benefitted from the prowess of Irish athletes too: South Africa was represented by Kennedy McArthur, an Antrim man, in the 1912 Olympic Games. He won the gold in the marathon with a time of just over two hours thirty-six minutes, especially impressive given the temperatures of well over 30 degrees in which he was running. Peter O'Connor was one athlete who was determined to represent

Ireland. He won a gold medal at the 1906 Athens Intercalated Olympics in the triple jump, while also taking the silver medal in the long jump. Although officially forced to compete for Britain, nationalist O'Connor smuggled in an Irish flag and had it erected for the presentation. He will go down as the first man in history to raise an Irish flag at the Olympics.

A newly independent Ireland would win occasional medals at the Olympics. At its first games in 1924, Oliver St John Gogarty won a bronze medal in the now long-abolished literature category for his poem 'Ode to the Tailteann Games'. The country did not win gold medals with regularity, however, and between 1960 and 1992, they won none at all. This makes it even more remarkable that on 1 August 1932, the country won two gold medals in just over an hour in Los Angeles. Ireland, in very poor economic circumstances, sent only four track and field athletes, all of whom had to endure a nearly two-week journey by various means of transport. One of these athletes was Dr Pat O'Callaghan, a native of Cork. O'Callaghan had previously been the youngest medical graduate in Ireland but was also highly regarded as an athlete, excelling in various sports. In 1925, he became interested in hammer throwing. Unable to afford the expensive equipment at the time, it is said that O'Callaghan took an old cannonball from a nearby abandoned castle and attached a handle, training by throwing it in local fields. His perseverance paid off, and he won several national competitions, astonishing seasoned throwers who had never heard of him. Bob Tisdall was another unknown athlete at the time, born in Sri Lanka to Irish parents. He moved to Tipperary at the age of 5 and developed into a talented athlete in various disciplines. In 1932, Tisdall applied for an Irish Olympic trial for the 400m hurdles, despite having never competed in the event before. He trained by jumping over timbers he had borrowed from a local yard. Nevertheless, he earned a spot on Ireland's small Olympic team.

On 1 August, both men faced daunting challenges. Tisdall, in particular, was up against several well-known competitors, including the previous two Olympic champions. However, against all odds, Tisdall led the race from start to finish, and despite striking the final hurdle with his foot, he managed to maintain his lead and finish in record time, much to the crowd's astonishment. Rather than basking in his victory, Tisdall rushed off the track, brushing aside eager journalists, to find his teammate Pat O'Callaghan, who had discovered that his only pair of spiked shoes had spikes that were too long, causing them to stick to the turf and negatively affect his throw. Tisdall and O'Callaghan quickly used a hacksaw to trim down the spikes. This adjustment worked, and O'Callaghan's final throw went over 176ft, securing him the gold medal. Unsurprisingly, the two men were celebrated as national heroes. When they returned to Ireland, they were greeted by thousands of spectators and they took part in a 9-mile parade through Dublin, with crowds cheering all the way. Though both were reportedly offered Hollywood movie contracts, neither accepted. The newly independent Irish Free State, still politically divided and struggling financially in its first decade, found great unity in the achievements of these two sportsmen, who, with little training and basic equipment, defeated the best athletes in the world.

8

Unlikely Arts, Music and Culture

Remarkable Irish Musicians

Ireland takes its music so seriously that it is the only country in the world with a musical instrument as its national symbol, a harp. The harp can be seen on all government documents in Ireland and it is always left facing. On pints of Guinness, on the other hand, the harp faces to the right.

Ireland has been producing fantastic musicians for millennia and many instruments from Bronze Age times have been recovered in the country. The Celts, too, played a variety of horns and whistles, as well as the harp. Turlough O'Carolan, 'the last of the Irish Bards', is among Ireland's most famous, and most revered, musicians and his style may have been influenced by the ancient music of pre-historic Ireland. Born in Co. Meath in 1670, O'Carolan wrote and composed countless songs, many of which survive to this day and have been covered by modern bands such as Planxty and The Dubliners. What is particularly remarkable about O'Carolan was that he had been blinded by smallpox at the age of 18. This did not deter him from embarking on a half-century of travelling the country as a poet and musician, however. He sang and recited his own compositions to rapt audiences and his fame grew far and wide. O'Carolan became a common visitor to wealthy homes, where his skills were much in demand. He died in 1738 and, today, many consider him to be Ireland's national composer. Anthony Raftery was of a similar vein. Despite also being blind, Raftery travelled extensively throughout the west of Ireland, visiting homes to perform music and recite his own poems before his death in 1835. Due to his blindness, Raftery never wrote down his compositions. Thankfully, some contemporaries recorded them, and his works are still celebrated today.

Ireland continues to produce many singers and musicians that make their mark on the world stage today. Obvious examples in recent years across various genres include Fontaines D.C., Snow Patrol, U2, The Cranberries, Enya, Westlife and Bob Geldof, the latter being as well known for his mammoth fundraising efforts for charity in the form of Live Aid as he is for his music with the Boomtown Rats. There were also many world-famous stars over the centuries who are less well remembered today. One of them was John McCormack, a native of Athlone, whose singing astonished all who knew him from a young age. Born in 1884, McCormack received his operatic training in Italy and, in the gramophone age, was the Elvis Presley of his day, playing to packed concert halls in countries all around the globe. He was made a papal count in 1928 due to his dedication to charity work.

Count John McCormack taking time out of singing to enjoy a game of tennis. (Library of Congress)

He was not the only Irish musician with Italian training. Margaret Burke Sheridan, born in Castlebar to a postmaster, also exhibited great talent and after a chance meeting with Guglielmo Marconi, the famous inventor, she was gifted a trip to Italy to learn opera from the best teachers in the world. She was considered top class, even in such a discerning country when it comes to the art of opera singing, and Burke Sheridan sang in operas all over the world, being at the height of her powers in the early 1920s. Catherine Hayes, a Limerick woman born in 1818, also made her mark on the world of opera, perfecting her craft in France and Italy. She would come to be known as the Irish Nightingale.

Patrick Sarsfield Gilmore was another musician who made an indelible mark on world music. A native of Co. Galway, he emigrated to America in 1847 aged 18. Having learned the cornet at a young age, Gilmore quickly got work in a music shop in Boston before joining the city's brass band. His talent was unmistakable and he enlisted in the Northern Army in the American Civil War, during which he published the words and music for 'When Johnny Comes Marching Home', a song that soon grew to national prominence. Gilmore became famous throughout America and in 1869 he organised an enormous peace jubilee aimed at uniting the country after the war. It featured an orchestra of 1,000 musicians, conducted by Gilmore himself, and hundreds of thousands of spectators were present. Gilmore died suddenly while touring in 1892 but is still remembered, in Ireland and in America, as a pioneering musician who escaped the Famine and changed the course of musical history.

Ireland has given much to the world musically and the world has often reciprocated. Handel's *Messiah*, considered one of the greatest oratorios ever written, premiered in Dublin in April 1742, possibly on Friday the thirteenth, although this did not bring bad luck in this case. Irish artists have also won the Eurovision Song Contest seven times, the joint highest number of any country. This included four successes in five years between 1992 and 1996. The country may have also have produced the most famous Christmas song of all time in the shape of 'Fairytale of New York'. Now considered a timeless classic, The Pogues and Kirsty McColl's 1987 hit was nevertheless kept off the UK Christmas Number 1 spot by the Pet Shop Boys' cover 'Always on my Mind'.

Strange Stories of Irish Film and Television

Ireland has acted as the backdrop to many international blockbusters. The first American film to be filmed outside the United States was the 1910 feature *The Lad from Old Ireland*. The twelve-minute silent movie, partly filmed on location in Kerry, tells the story of a poor Irish farmer named Terry who travels to America leaving his love behind. Many later films would use Ireland as a backdrop, perhaps most famously *The Quiet Man*, a film starring John Wayne as a retired boxer, Sean Thornton, haunted by his past. He travels to the fictional town of Innisfree in Ireland and buys a house before falling for Mary Kate Danaher, played by Maureen O'Hara. The west of Ireland was the backdrop of the film, director John Ford having strong family connections locally, and the filming was done over six weeks in the summer of 1951. One grumble of the cast was the lack of modern conveniences in Ireland at the time. None of the pubs offered ice for their drinks, one publican reportedly telling a crew member, 'What's the use of ice? It will only melt anyway.' In the aftermath of the film's release, thousands of tourists, particularly Americans, visited the setting of the film, and villages such as Cong continue to benefit.

Braveheart was also largely filmed on location in Ireland in 1994, as the landscape was so similar to that of neighbouring Scotland that it could easily substitute as a backdrop. The Wicklow Mountains featured regularly, as did the plains of Meath and the magnificent Anglo-Norman castle at Trim, which doubled as the city of York. *Star Wars: The Last Jedi* made great use of Ireland's incredible landscape. Coastal areas were showcased, especially the magnificent Skellig Islands off Kerry and the area around Brow Head in Co. Cork. The Skelligs doubled as Temple Island, with Luke Skywalker living there in exile. The island was ideal for the lonely, remote yet stunning area the filmmakers wished to convey and led to an explosion of interest in the islands among tourists.

In 1997, *Saving Private Ryan* was filmed on the east coast, using the beautiful sandy expanse of Curracloe Beach, Co. Wexford, as the setting for Omaha Beach, so critical during the D-Day landings of 1944. Hundreds of Irish extras can be seen storming the beaches in the film. *Harry Potter and the Half-Blood Prince* from 2009 was filmed partly on location at the Cliffs of Moher in Co. Clare, while part of the tearjerker *Marley and Me* also used the west of Ireland as a backdrop when Owen Wilson and Jennifer Anniston went to Ireland on their honeymoon. *Ryan's Daughter* was filmed on the Dingle Peninsula in 1969, an entire village being built as a set. The crew of 200 spent the winter filming in the rural locale with world-famous director David Lean and the film's biggest star, Robert Mitchum, being particularly popular in the locality. Interestingly, the romantic western *Far and Away*, famous for its dodgy Irish accents, was also filmed near Dingle in the 1990s and it, too, had a village built specially for the set.

Ireland has made its mark on the world of acting over the centuries too. Many will know of Colin Farrell, Pierce Brosnan and Maureen O'Hara but fewer will be familiar with Ada Rehan, one of the most critically acclaimed actresses in the nineteenth century, particularly in Shakespearean plays. She was born Bridie Crehan in Limerick in 1857, and grew to be arguably the most loved actress in America in the closing decades of the nineteenth century. Dubliner Angela Greene was a big star in Hollywood in the 1930s and '40s, as was Maureen O'Sullivan, a Roscommon native who appeared in movies such as *Tarzan*. She was also the mother of Mia Farrow, herself an acclaimed actress. Grace Kelly, one of the most famous actresses of the twentieth century, who went on to become the Princess of Monaco, was an American but of Irish descent, her grandfather having departed Newport, Co. Mayo, in the late 1880s. The princess visited Mayo for the first time in 1961, eventually buying her grandfather's ruined former house and land in 1976. She afterwards spent many holidays in the area and it was rumoured that she was going to build a holiday home on the site of her grandfather's homestead, a plan that could not come to fruition due to her tragic death in a car crash in 1982. At her funeral, wildflowers from the fields around her ancestral home were collected into a wreath and displayed.

In terms of television, Ireland's national broadcaster, Raidió Teilifís Éireann, was set up in 1961, although those living in the north of Ireland and on the east coast could get the BBC channels on their television sets long before that date. Throughout the 1950s, there was a growing clamour for a dedicated Irish television service, although the conservative government of the day rejected the idea, labelling television as merely a 'luxury service' that was largely undesirable to the public. A government committee in the mid-1950s criticised British programming

Grace Kelly. (Library of Congress)

as being overly frank about sexual matters and too deferential to the British Royal Family. Nevertheless, thousands of Irish people owned television sets and watched such programming, and as the 1950s wore on, it became increasingly clear that television was here to stay. This caused the government to reluctantly set in train the foundation of RTÉ, which first broadcast to the public on New Year's Eve, 1961. In his opening address, Taoiseach Éamon de Valera lamented:

> I must admit that sometimes when I think of television and radio and their immense power, I feel somewhat afraid. Like atomic energy, it can be used for incalculable good but it can also do irreparable harm. Never was there in the hands of men an instrument so powerful to influence the thoughts and actions of the multitude. It can lead through demoralisation to decadence and dissolution.[15]

The first programme, a gala show countdown to the new year, featured guests such as Archbishop of Armagh John D'Alton, who warned parents not to allow their children to become television addicts. The early days of television in Ireland featured a huge amount of religious programming but there were other more secular items, including *The Late Late Show*, today considered to be the longest-running live talk show in the world, having been first broadcast in 1962. Hosted by Gay Byrne, the chat show quickly gained popularity among viewers and did not shy from hosting discussions on controversial and taboo topics in Irish society. There were several scandals that today seem quaint. One of the most prominent was a light-hearted quiz aired in February 1966 that ignited tensions between the Catholic hierarchy in Ireland and RTÉ. The 'Bishop and the Nightie' episode, as it was dubbed, involved Dublin couple Eileen and Richard,

---

15 RTÉ Archives, Media, Opening Night President's Address.

who were members of the audience that took part in a quiz for married couples. One of the questions asked Eileen about the colour of the nightie she wore on her honeymoon. This segment sparked a strong reaction from Dr Thomas Ryan, the Bishop of Clonfert, who condemned the question as 'most objectionable'. Gay Byrne acknowledged that the quiz had been 'embarrassing to some viewers' and expressed regret if that was the case. Others were perplexed at the bishop's strong reaction to a very mundane question. Another scandal occurred in 1985, when Byrne interviewed two lesbian ex-nuns while a protest was waged outside the studio. The two Americans, Nancy Manahan and Rosemary Curb, were in Ireland to promote their book *Breaking Silence: Lesbian Nuns on Convent Sexuality*, and the episode was said to have had exceptionally high ratings despite, or perhaps because of, the controversy.

Irish Literature

Ireland has, of course, produced many renowned writers, poets and artists. It even has a claim to some writers more commonly associated with Britain. One of these is the author of the *The Chronicles of Narnia*, C.S. Lewis, who was born in Belfast despite spending much of his life in England. He was proud of his Irish roots and never forgot the land of his birth. The area around Co. Down was said to have inspired Narnia. Likewise, the Burren in Co. Clare may have been an inspiration for J.R.R. Tolkien's Middle-earth in *The Lord of the Rings*.

The quintessentially English writers the Brontë sisters also have a strong Irish connection. Anne, Charlotte and Emily Brontë's father, Patrick, was born in Co. Down in 1777, the eldest of ten children. His surname at birth was Prunty and he was academically talented. He worked as a private tutor before enrolling in

The Burren, which was believed to have inspired Tolkien's Middle-earth. (Photograph by the author)

Cambridge University, a rare accomplishment for an Irishman at the time. Charlotte, in particular, loved her father's homeland, and honeymooned there with her Irish husband, Arthur Bell Nicholls.

Some Irish writers were less impressed with their homeland than Charlotte Brontë. James Joyce famously described Ireland as 'the old sow that eats her farrow'. The playwright J.M. Synge may have agreed. His work *The Playboy of the Western World* caused a riot in the Abbey Theatre in 1907 when the audience decreed that it gave an unfavourable account of Irish life. History repeated itself in 1926 when Seán O'Casey's *The Plough and the Stars* was performed at the same venue. The play centred around the Easter Rising but the audience, which included some widows of the leaders of the 1916 Rising, booed at what they saw as an unflattering distortion of the event. This caused an outraged W.B. Yeats to stand and address the audience, saying: 'You have disgraced yourselves again. Is this to be an ever-recurring celebration of the arrival of Irish genius?'

Nevertheless, many Irishmen and women have become successful writers and artists and several have won Nobel Prizes in various artistic fields. W.B. Yeats himself famously took the award for literature in 1923, just as the new nation was finding its feet, a huge achievement in difficult times. Playwright George Bernard Shaw was next to claim the honour two years later, following it with an Oscar in 1938. He did not enjoy the trappings of such ceremonies, however, and turned down many such awards and much of the money that went with them. The playwright, best known for *Pygmalion* and *Major Barbara*, was often a critic of the establishment and a man blessed with incredible wit. One famous tale about Shaw concerns a supposed conversation he had with a beautiful actress, who said to him 'Might we have a child together? Imagine, with my beauty and your brains what it could be.' Shaw allegedly responded, 'Indeed, but what if it ended up with my beauty and your brains?' Shaw variously denied and admitted this tale. The playwright and novelist of high renown, Samuel Beckett, who lived much of his life in France, received the Nobel Prize for Literature in 1969, while the Derry native Seamus Heaney also captured the award. Heaney was much loved in his home country, despite spending many years living in America, where his poetry was oft-quoted by American presidents.

Irish Art

Irish art goes back millennia, from Stone Age carvings at Newgrange to the distinctive Celtic La Tène style, famous for its curvilinear lines. The Corleck Head is a fine example of Celtic art. It is a stone idol with three faces that was discovered in Co. Cavan in 1855 and probably originates from the second century. It appears to be a homage to a Celtic god, whose identity is today a mystery. The head was dug up by a local farmer, who kept it in his home for decades. It was later placed on top of a gatepost, where it was recognised by a folklore researcher as an important piece in the 1930s, some eighty years after its rediscovery. Christian monks also created stunning artwork within their manuscripts, as can famously be seen in the *Book of Kells*. They also erected ornate stone crosses, such as the high cross at Monasterboice, Co. Louth, with pictures and carvings depicting religious stories.

Ornate high crosses such as this one can be found all over Ireland. (Photograph by the author)

In more recent centuries, Ireland has had many artists of renown. Francis Bacon, the figurative painter, was born in Ireland but spent most of his life in England. Other famous Irish painters include Paul Henry, the Belfast-born landscape painter, who captured the west of Ireland spectacularly in his work. Paul and his wife Grace lived on Achill Island, Co. Mayo, for close to a decade, and Grace was an equally talented artist whose works are included in major collections in Ireland and abroad.

John Lavery was an Irish artist with a fascinating back story. Born in Belfast, he was orphaned at a young age and ran away to Scotland as a boy. Despite this difficult start in life, he was an immensely talented painter and was internationally famous by the first decade of the twentieth century. Lavery was particularly adept at portraits and was tasked with painting major figures in political and religious life, both in Ireland and abroad.

He was even commissioned to paint the British Royal Family, for which he was paid £2,000. Lavery is as famous for whom he married as for his paintings; Hazel Martyn, later Lady Lavery, became his wife in 1909. Hazel was an artist herself who came to be well known in British and Irish high society and she seems to have been having an affair with the austere Irish politician Kevin O'Higgins throughout the 1920s. Hazel was also a personal friend of Michael Collins, the Irish rebel, and he also seems to have been infatuated with her. It was John Lavery who painted Collins' famous posthumous portrait as he lay dead in the mortuary chapel in Dublin, a work that can be viewed in the Hugh Lane Gallery to this day. Hazel Lavery, meanwhile, posed for the figure that could be seen on all Irish banknotes for several decades.

Several Irish artists even made their mark on the Olympics. Art was a discipline between 1912 and 1948, although the artwork had to be an original piece and be inspired by a sporting event. Jack B. Yeats, brother of William, won independent Ireland's first medal, a silver, at the 1924 Games for his painting of the Liffey Swim, an annual sporting event in Dublin. Twenty-four years later, Meath native Letitia Hamilton won a bronze medal for her painting, 'The Meath Hunt: Point-to-Point Races'. Strangely, the whereabouts of this award-winning piece are unknown today. It was not the only painting to go missing. Aloysius O'Kelly's 'Mass in a Connemara Cabin' is a striking piece that features people in prayer as the priest says a station Mass. It was the only Irish painting ever exhibited in the famous Paris Salon but disappeared mysteriously around 1895, when O'Kelly emigrated to America. There was speculation as to its whereabouts but it did not re-emerge until 2002, when it was discovered in the presbytery of St Patrick's Church in the Cowgate district of Edinburgh. It had been hanging on the wall of a parochial house for decades, its value unnoticed by the occupants until an eagle-eyed visitor urged them to consult an art expert, who confirmed it was an original O'Kelly. Some sources suggest that the painting had been a present from the artist to a priest, Canon Hannon. It now hangs in the National Gallery of Ireland and is worth over €500,000.

It is difficult to pick Ireland's most influential painting, although 'An Allegory' by Seán Keating, a bitter satire of the Irish Civil War painted in 1924, the year after the conflict concluded, is surely a contender. Frederic William Burton's 'Meeting on a Turret Stairs', which was voted Ireland's favourite painting in 2012, is also highly regarded. Many famous foreign paintings also hang in the National Gallery of Ireland. 'The Taking of Christ' by Caravaggio, a painting depicting the arrest of Christ after the Last Supper, may be the best known, but there are also works by Peter Paul Rubens and Johannes Vermeer.

Language in Ireland

Ireland's linguistic history is complicated. We do not know for sure what language the earliest Irish people spoke, but we do know that the Celts brought a language with them that is a forerunner of the modern Irish language and this may have fused somewhat with whatever language was there before. When the Vikings arrived, they spoke Old Norse for centuries, while many of the early Norman visitors to Ireland spoke French, particularly the elites. English, meanwhile, became the lingua franca of the Pale, the area around Dublin, for centuries after the Norman invasion, but it would take far longer for it to spread across the country, where Irish remained the mother tongue of most. In Co. Wicklow, it is believed that native Irish was extinct as early as 1830. Conversely, the 1911 census still recorded Irish as being very strong in many western districts and there remained some Irish speakers in these areas who recorded that they had no grasp of English whatsoever.

The decline of the Irish language was a slow process that accelerated rapidly in the nineteenth century. In 1800, for example, there were more Irish speakers worldwide than speakers of Swedish, Finnish or Dutch. The causes of this rapid decline were numerous. First, the Great Famine hit the poorer, Irish-speaking western regions hardest. Additionally, in a country where emigration was often the expected fate for young adults, English was viewed as essential, while Irish was seen as a hindrance. There was also widespread negative sentiment towards the language among many clergy in the Catholic Church and politicians like Daniel O'Connell. Furthermore, most schools did not teach Irish at all during this time and British officials insisted that all business be carried out in English. These factors collectively reinforced the view that English was a symbol of progress and modernity, while Irish was seen as outdated. Not everyone felt this way. Thomas Davis, a contemporary of O'Connell in Famine-era Ireland, famously stated that, 'A nation should guard its language more than its territories – 'tis a surer barrier, and more important frontier, than fortress or river.' It would take an awakening of interest in Irish culture at the end of the nineteenth century, and the founding of Conradh na Gaeilge in 1893, to spread this viewpoint far and wide.

Irish today can be broadly divided into Ulster, Connacht and Munster dialects, and remains spoken as a community language in parts of seven counties: Galway, Mayo, Donegal, Kerry, Cork, Waterford and Meath. Meath, the only county not situated on the south-west or west coast, is perhaps the most interesting of these. One of the main aims of the new Irish state in 1922 had been the restoration of the Irish language nationwide, a tough challenge in a country that had been largely forced to adopt English as the spoken tongue in the century before independence. The province of Leinster had virtually no Irish-speaking areas at all by 1925 and, consequently, a transfer of people from Gaeltacht areas in the west to Co. Meath in the

1930s and '40s was inaugurated. Meath had many large landed estates that were to be broken up after independence and it was decided that as many Irish speakers as practicable would be chosen, with the successful applicants being given a new land commission house, 22 acres of land, a horse, a cow, poultry and an allowance of 30 shillings a week for one year. Large families were encouraged. It proved a success and has left a thriving Irish language community based around the village of Rath Chairn, hundreds of miles from the other Gaeltachtaí.

Other Languages and Dialects

Ireland has also been home to other dialects and languages over the centuries, some of which are barely remembered today. One of these is Yola, an ancient dialect of middle English that was spoken in the south-eastern part of Ireland, notably the southern baronies of Forth and Bargy in Co. Wexford. Yola itself comes from the word 'Old'. It seems to have originated with the Normans in the twelfth century, and remained largely unchanged with a smattering of French, Irish and even Flemish words. It was distinctive from English for many centuries but died out in the mid-nineteenth century. Fingallian was another dialect spoken in North Dublin that had much in common with Yola. Some examples of Yola words were 'farthoo', which means 'why'; 'betweesk', which means 'between'; and 'fornint', meaning 'in front of'. Ulster Scots is another dialect of Ireland. Spoken in the province of Ulster, it has many similarities with the English spoken in the Lowlands of Scotland. It came across with the plantation of Ulster and many of its words have passed into everyday English, including 'gab', which means to talk; 'dally', which means to dawdle; and 'blether', which means to talk nonsense. Irish travellers also have a unique language that is often called Cant, but also De Gamman or Shelta. Shelta may come from the Irish verb 'siúil', which means to walk. It has many words that come from old Irish and is often not intelligible for those who only speak English or Irish. Words in Shelta include 'kam' for son and 'gruber' for work.

Hiberno-English is the primary language spoken in Ireland today, however, and its accent and cadence are completely different than English spoken anywhere else. The country has also offered many words to the English language, 'boycott' being one excellent example. The word 'quiz' may also have originated in Ireland. One popular myth suggests that a theatre manager from Dublin named Richard Daly made a bet that he could introduce a new word into English within twenty-four hours. He chose the meaningless 'quiz' as this new word, paying a group of street children to write it on walls throughout the city. There are many others. 'Galore' comes from the Irish word 'go leor', meaning 'many'. 'Whiskey' is from the Irish words 'Uisce Beatha', meaning 'water of life'. 'Gob', 'limerick', 'hooligan', 'bog', 'tory' and 'slogan' are other words believed to have originated in Ireland that have gone far beyond our shores at this point. The word 'yahoo', to describe a rude or violent person, is also of Irish origin and originally described a fictional race in Jonathan Swift's *Gulliver's Travels*. The phrase 'Beyond the Pale' is undoubtedly of Irish origin and refers to the areas beyond Dublin that were once considered barbarous. And what of the word 'lynch'? One theory traces its origin back to 1493, when a young Spanish nobleman named Gomez was allegedly murdered by the son of James Lynch Fitzstephen, the mayor of Galway. In a dramatic display of justice, the mayor is said to have hanged his own son from a window on Market Street in the city to demonstrate that the law applied equally to all. Over time, many have assumed that the verb 'to lynch' derives from this story, though there are other theories as to its origin.

9
Strange Moments of Irish History

Irish Famine

When one thinks of Ireland and famine, the 1840s spring to mind, although an equally devastating but less well-documented famine occurred in the early 1740s. The year 1740 was savagely cold right up until the summer, and many animals died in the fields while the harvest was below even the minimal subsistence rate. The weather in the first half of 1741 was equally savage and up to 15 per cent of Ireland's 2.5 million people may have died in this period. Other mini-famines occurred afterwards, notably in 1822 and 1831, but none would be as devastating as that which occurred between 1845 and 1851 when blight struck the potato crop.

Queen Victoria.

One strange aspect of the Great Famine was the identity of those who gave money to the starving Irish. It is a myth that Queen Victoria gave just £5. She donated closer to £2,000 from her personal resources. The British government response was sadly inadequate, however. The workhouse was their main means of dealing with the starving poor, although this option was made as unattractive to the starving masses as possible. All land above a quarter acre had to be forfeited before entry and each family was split up on arrival and forced to perform hard labour to earn the scanty meals provided by the dreaded institution. Senior British figures with responsibility for Ireland, such as Charles Trevelyan, considered the Famine 'providence' sent by God and it was left to other groupings to try and alleviate the terrible suffering.

The Quakers did more than their fair share, setting up soup kitchens throughout the country. Asenath Nicholson, an American author and philanthropist, offered all the assistance she could as she travelled around Ireland in the 1840s, bequeathing money and food to as many as possible. Incidentally, Nicholson was probably the author of the world's first vegetarian cookbook. The freed African-American slave and activist Frederick Douglass also came to Ireland as the Great Famine took hold. He was appalled by the conditions in Ireland but equally amazed by his ability to fraternise freely with white people, in a way that would have been unthinkable in America at that time.

In a striking act of generosity, the Choctaw and Cherokee nations, despite having recently been displaced from their ancestral lands, also contributed $800 to the cause. This gesture has not been forgotten and today the Irish State offers scholarships to students from these tribes to come to Ireland to study as a thanks for the benevolence of their ancestors. The Sultan of the Ottoman Empire also showed great support, donating £1,000 and sending five shiploads of food. Drogheda in Co. Louth received much of this aid and the town's coat of arms has a crescent and star on it, widely believed to be an acknowledgment of such generosity. However, in all likelihood, this symbol comes from the arms of King John, who presented Drogheda with its first charter in 1210.

Famine follies were another bizarre, if well-meant, aspect of Irish famines. These were buildings that served no real purpose but were built as projects to provide labour for the starving masses, usually by local landlords. These follies often took the form of a pillar, grotto or temple of some sort. Hussey's Folly near Dingle, Co. Kerry, is one example. It was built early in the Great Famine and was named after a local land agent. Resembling a watch tower, it has no discernible purpose. Another famous example of a folly is in The Neale, Co. Mayo. It is a large 30ft stone monument that was built in the shape of a pyramid. It stands to this day. The Jealous Wall in Co. Westmeath is the largest folly in Ireland. Built by Robert Rochfort, it was intended to resemble the artificial ruin of an abbey and to block from Robert's view the sight of his brother's grand residence, of which he was said to be jealous!

The ordinary people of Ireland had far more pressing concerns than jealousy and the population of the country plummeted during the Famine years. One million deaths occurred, while another 1.5 million deserted the country for foreign shores. There was anger against the authorities and occasional food riots but the only rebellion of sorts, occurring in 1848, was doomed to failure. The starving Irish were in no position to resist the armed forces of Britain and the Young Ireland Movement's attempt to overthrow the British government was derisively known as 'The Battle of Widow McCormack's Cabbage Patch', and petered out after barely a day. Despite this, the British were angered and the sentences handed out to the conspirators were harsh in the extreme. Leaders such as Thomas Francis Meagher and William Smith O'Brien were sentenced to be hanged, drawn and quartered. These sentences were eventually commuted to transportation when cooler heads prevailed.

The most astonishing aspect of the rebellion is the ultimately successful fate of the transported rebel leaders: Thomas Francis Meagher became governor of the American territory (later state) of Montana; John Mitchel became editor of the *New York Daily News*; Charles Gavan Duffy was voted in as premier of the Australian state of Victoria; Thomas D'Arcy McGee rose to become the minister of agriculture in the Canadian government. James Stephens, meanwhile, stayed true to his principles and founded the Irish Republican Brotherhood, an organisation that would ultimately play a huge role in securing Irish independence.

The Famine ended in 1851, but its legacy cast a long shadow. A deep gloom fell over the people, even well after the crisis ended, as John O'Rourke remembered fifty years later:

> When the Famine had abated in intensity, a priest was one day in a field which was separated from the public road by a wall. He heard a voice on the road; it was that of a peasant girl humming a song. The tears rushed to his eyes. He walked quickly towards her, searching meantime for some coin to give her. He placed a shilling in her hand, with a feeling somewhat akin to enthusiasm. 'It was,' said he 'the first joyous sound I had heard for six months.'[16]

The Land War

The Famine thinned out the Irish population, killed off the Irish language in many parts of the country and left many Irish people broken spirited, destitute or scattered to the four corners of the globe. Nevertheless, a spirit of rebellion remained and, in the decades afterwards, there would be two uprisings. The first, a Fenian revolt in 1867, was largely a failure. Prolonged heavy snow in the week leading up to the event hampered plans to rebel, while an

16 O'Rourke, J., *History of the Irish Famine* (1902), p.221.

informer named John Joseph Croydon spilled plans concerning the rebellion to police, so they were aware of what was going to happen. The rebellion did go ahead, with thousands of Fenians assembling in Dublin, Cork and Drogheda, but it lasted barely a day and the leaders were rounded up and captured.

A far more successful revolution was the Land War from 1879–81. The Land League, founded in 1879, truly united Irish farmers and the war combined violence with non-violent tactics such as boycotting. The mastermind of the Land League was Michael Davitt, a man whose family had been evicted from their Co. Mayo home during the Famine and forced to move to Lancashire, England. He remembered this moment bitterly:

> Failing to wipe off all arrears, we were one morning thrown out on the roadside and our little house and home pulled down before our eyes by the reigning institution: the 'Crowbar Brigade.' I was then but four and a half years old, yet I have a distinct remembrance of that morning's scene. The remnant of our household furniture flung about the road, the roof of our house falling in and the thatch taking fire, my mother and father looking on with four young children.[17]

The Land War probably would never have happened if it had not been for Davitt but it also owed something to heavy rain. Rain is, of course, a reality all over Ireland, but one of the wettest years in recent centuries was 1878, when crops were destroyed and sodden grain lay in the fields. It also led to waterlogged turf that would not burn. The following year was little better and this terrible spell of weather led to real fears of another famine. The Land League was established in response and it demanded better conditions for tenant farmers, in protests that led to the violence of the Land War and ultimately the redistribution of

---

17 Davitt, M., *Jottings in Solitary* (2003), p.6.

Irish land. Rather than relying on violence alone, the Land War spurred the people into using a new tactic that would ultimately give the world a new word. A Co. Mayo land agent named Charles Boycott refused to lower rents in the Land War and was 'boycotted'. The locals refused to serve him, work for him, talk to him or aid him in any way. Boycott was forced to pay thousands of pounds for labourers from the north to harvest his crops, making his farm enterprise a failure. Boycott left the area and the tactic caught on, as did the word. This action proved inspired and forced the British government to alter land legislation in favour of tenant farmers.

A strange happening during the Land War, although not directly related to the conflict, was a religious apparition that was said to have occurred at the small village of Knock, Co. Mayo, on 21 August 1879. Fifteen individuals saw a vision of Mary, St Joseph, St John, a lamb, and a cross on an altar on the gable wall of the church in their local village. The apparition allegedly continued for a full two hours. This miracle would eventually get the sanction of Rome and the basilica that was later built at Knock is visited by over a million pilgrims annually. Pope John Paul II's visit to Ireland in September 1979 included a trip to Knock, as did the visit of Pope Francis in 2018.

The First World War and the Easter Rising

Ireland went through a tumultuous period between 1914 and 1923 with the First World War, the Easter Rising, the War of Independence and then the Civil War following one after another. Although the First World War was largely ignored in Irish history books for decades after independence, approximately 200,000 Irishmen served in the British armed forces and some 50,000 were killed. Many of these soldiers believed that they were fighting for the freedom of small nations, as the British government regularly claimed, an assertion that was backed by many of Ireland's foremost politicians, including John Redmond, whose own brother would die on the front line. Ireland played its part in the British war effort in other ways. Dubliner Walter Gordon Wilson invented the tank, something that changed the trajectory of the war in Britain's favour.

Lord Horatio Kitchener, whose image appeared on the most famous recruitment poster of the First World War, his index finger pointing to the viewer with the caption 'Your Country Needs You', was also an Irishman, even if he did not generally highlight the fact and had little sympathy for the Irish who desired home rule. He was among Britain's most high-profile war casualties when the ship he was travelling on ran into a German mine in 1916. The island of Ireland even became a theatre of war briefly in May 1918, when Portballintrae in Co. Antrim was shelled from the sea. The village was not the intended target, however. A steamer called SS *Wheater* was in the sea just off the coast when it encountered a U-boat, which opened fire. Thirteen shells missed the ship and hit the village instead. A cow was the only fatality on land. Another tragedy on Irish soil occurred in 1917 when a German barrel mine that had floated onto a beach at Inverin, Co. Galway, exploded, killing nine local men.

As the deaths in the First World War mounted, the 1916 Easter Rising was declared by a committed group of Irish nationalists, determined that Ireland should make a strike for independence. Not all the fighters were Irish, however. James Connolly, one of the executed leaders, was a Scotsman. Englishmen also fought in the General Post Office, Dublin, including a man nicknamed 'Blimey' due to his thick Cockney accident. Even more surprising fighters in the GPO were two Scandinavian men, a Swede and a Finn. The men had arrived to Dublin on a ship and were in the city by chance when the fighting broke out. They were admitted to the building when they told Captain Liam Tannam that they wished to fight for Ireland, a small nation like their own, under the yoke of a foreign oppressor. The rebels stood little chance, however, something the leader Patrick Pearse understood well, although he viewed it as a strike against Britain and something that could change the mindset of the people of Ireland in the long term. British reinforcements flooded into the city on gunboats up the Liffey and turned the tide of battle, although not before they struck dozens of empty buildings, almost destroying Liberty Hall, which was completely devoid of rebels.

This strike against the British Army when they were at war was considered in Westminster as a great betrayal. Many Irish themselves were horrified by the stand taken in Dublin, and the rebels were pelted with vegetables by some Dubliners after their arrests. Many newspapers also tripped over themselves to condemn the reckless action. As the executions of the leaders of the Rising continued, public anger started to wane and turn towards the British government and their merciless reprisal policy. Some newspapers took longer to change their perspective. On 12 May, the *Irish Independent* called for the execution of the only two leaders who had yet to be shot by firing squad, James Connolly and Seán Mac Diarmada. The former was critically injured while the latter suffered from polio. The newspaper nevertheless described how they 'played a more sinister part in the campaign than those who have already been punished with severity and it would hardly be fair to treat these leniently because the cry for clemency has been raised ... Let the worst of the ringleaders be singled out and dealt with as they deserve.'[18]

Both were executed on the day the article was published, Connolly being forced to sit on a wooden box as he was unfit to stand. Stories of Joseph Plunkett marrying his lover Grace Gifford in a prison cell hours before his execution also emerged,

---

18 *Irish Independent*, 12 May 1916.

increasing the sympathy for the rebels. The Rising was ultimately crushed but nationalist feeling continued to grow, eventually uniting most, although certainly not all, Irish people in a desire for independence.

The War of Independence and the Civil War

The change in the Irish mindset was shown clearly in the 1918 election when the pro-independence Sinn Féin party, previously a fringe grouping, won the vast majority of seats, with the exception of north-east Ulster. The War of Independence began in earnest in January 1919 and saw unity among many people from all sides of the political spectrum. Kevin O'Higgins, who would go on to wryly suggest that he had fought with the 'most conservative-minded revolutionaries that ever put through a successful revolution', saw the fight for freedom through one lens, but many on the Left also fought for independence. There was even a short-lived 'Limerick Soviet' in April 1919 when workers from the county's trade unions protested over the arrest and subsequent shooting of a colleague who was a member of Sinn Fein. As his funeral approached, the British declared martial law in the city. The response was the calling of a general strike and the establishment of a 'Soviet' to manage the city's affairs. Limerick even briefly had its own currency and almost the entire city went on strike in an event that undermined British authority in the area.

Another interesting aspect of the republican forces was the preponderance of former members of the British armed forces. Tom Barry was a prime example. He had served with the British Army in Mesopotamia, later Iraq, returning in 1919 to a new Ireland on a seemingly unstoppable course for freedom. Barry embraced this new creed, although it was at odds with what he had previously fought for. He later lamented that he had no national consciousness before he left and his British service was motivated only by a desire to see the world and to hold a gun. On his return, he became arguably the most ruthless IRA commander in the country, with many of the most disastrous engagements of the War of Independence, from a Crown perspective, happening in his West Cork patch. He later summed up the common view of him among his enemies by saying:

> They said I was ruthless, daring, savage, bloodthirsty, even heartless. The clergy called me and my comrades murderers; but the British were met with their own weapons. They had gone in the mire to destroy us and our nation and down after them we had to go.[19]

Arguably the strangest occurrences of the war years were the Marian apparitions in Templemore, Co. Tipperary, which nearly led to dangerous consequences for the self-proclaimed witness, Jimmy Walsh. Sixteen-year-old Walsh claimed to have seen statues of the Virgin Mary weeping blood in the town during the autumn of 1920, as the War of Independence was reaching its most brutal phase. He also reported having been visited by visions of Mary, and even spoke of a holy well that had appeared in the floor of his bedroom. Rumours spread that increasing numbers of Virgin Mary statues throughout the town were shedding tears of blood. Crowds began to flock to Templemore, as many as 15,000 pilgrims a day when the story was at its height, each hoping to witness the phenomenon. These enormous numbers of visitors forced the local IRA to briefly suspend their operations against Crown forces. Both the local Catholic Church and the IRA soon grew suspicious of Walsh, who had begun accepting money for performing

19 Barry, T., *Guerilla Days in Ireland* (1949), p.45.

cures on pilgrims and had earned the nickname 'the Saint'. A local IRA commander, Jimmy Leahy, had him interrogated, later labelling him either 'mentally abnormal' or a 'hypocrite'. Meanwhile, one of the statues was sent to Michael Collins for inspection, who discovered that a mechanism had been installed to simulate bleeding. Fearing retribution from the IRA, Walsh is believed to have fled Ireland for Australia, where he assumed a new identity.

The War of Independence resumed its former ferocity and deaths mounted. The singer George O'Dowd, better known as Boy George, found out on the BBC's *Who Do You Think You Are?* programme that his grand-uncle, Thomas Bryan, was one of the 'Forgotten Ten' who had been executed on 14 March 1921 for his part in an ambush of a Royal Irish Constabulary patrol. Bryan was one of some 2,000 deaths that would only end with the truce in July 1921. Michael Collins then helped broker the Anglo-Irish Treaty, which divided Ireland in two and left Northern Ireland as a part of the United Kingdom and the Free State as a member of the British empire with partial independence. On the handover of Dublin Castle, the Lord Lieutenant, Lord Fitzalan, was said to have admonished Collins by saying, 'You are seven minutes late, Mr Collins.' Collins quipped back: 'We've been waiting over seven hundred years, you can have the seven minutes.'

The Treaty did not go far enough for many fighters and would result in the civil war, or in Irish, Cogadh na gCarad: the War of Friends. One of the biggest mysteries of the conflict centres around who fired the fatal bullet that killed Michael Collins when he was travelling through his home county of Cork in August 1922. This was among the most disturbed areas in Ireland during the civil war but Collins' party saw fit to stop at several public houses, delaying them. As Collins drove through the countryside, they found many local roads trenched and blockaded. The convoy stopped to ask directions but it transpired that the man they asked was a member of the local anti-Treaty IRA. He quickly informed local fighters of the presence of Collins, causing them to scramble together an ambush. When the government party ran into this group, Collins is said to have leapt from the car and begun firing. He was struck by a single bullet, which hit him in the head and killed him almost instantly. He was the only fatality that day. For many decades nobody knew who had fired the fatal shot, although military pension records now suggest that Dennis 'Sonny' O'Neill, an anti-Treaty IRA fighter and a former policeman in the Royal Irish Constabulary, may have been the marksman. Collins' body was brought by ship to Dublin, it being too dangerous to transport it by road. When he arrived there, tens of thousands of people, both pro- and anti-Treaty, lined the road to mourn the man who had been the most important driving force behind independence. The civil war came to an end in May 1923 when the republicans dumped arms and reluctantly settled for peace in a nation-state with which they were not entirely comfortable.

Independent Ireland 1923–49: The War on Sex

The state would prove to be a disappointment to many, with the first years marked by poverty and increased emigration. A brief famine in the west in 1924 was largely kept out of the newspapers due to the embarrassment it would cause the new state. The Free State also proved to be a strongly conservative one and many aspects of life would be in the sights of the new government. Sex was not generally a topic considered worthy of discussion in polite society in post-independence Ireland. Unmarried mothers were treated poorly by the new state and mother and baby homes, where unmarried or pregnant mothers were dispatched, and sometimes held for years, were present in the new state. Many women in that position, particularly those with little family support, ended up in these institutions until the late 1940s at least, and the babies were often forcibly adopted.

Such inconvenient truths were largely ignored, or even tacitly supported, by the media. Also ignored was the fact that in the years leading up to Irish independence, the area around Montgomery Street in Dublin, commonly known as 'The Monto', was home to one of the largest red-light districts in Europe. Before independence, it was often claimed that most of the customers visiting the prostitutes had been British soldiers, suggesting that prostitution was primarily a British issue and would fade in independent Ireland. This did not come to pass and intense efforts were made to rid the area of its undesirable activities. By 1925, the Legion of Mary had made inroads into the task of clearing the area of those offering or seeking gratification of this sort, although in that year a scandal would rock the country, showing the Free State that some of its own elites were far from pure.

On the evening of 8 June 1925, Dr Patrick Purcell and Garda Superintendent Leopold Dillon, both from Co. Wicklow, made their way to Dublin in the doctor's two-seater car. Both men were married, with the doctor having two children. The two drank heavily during their journey to Dublin, arriving at 6.30 p.m. and parting ways. Both spent the evening drinking and socialising with women, including sex workers. Later that night, a drunken Purcell complained angrily to two hackney drivers that a prostitute had stolen £11 from him. He vowed to 'do for her' if he found her, adding that if he could not locate her, he would 'find another and leave her in the country where she wouldn't be found'. By 1 a.m., Purcell and Dillon had reunited at the upscale Shelbourne Hotel.

The following morning, at 7.30 a.m., the body of a young woman was discovered at Ticknock Crossroads, approximately 7 miles from the city centre. She had been shot in the heart. The victim was soon identified as Honor Bright. A taxi driver later recalled seeing a two-seater sports car, with two male occupants, parked at Harold's Cross when he dropped Honor off. At the time, cars were scarce and easily identifiable, so the vehicle was quickly traced, leading to the arrest of Purcell and Dillon. They were identified by several witnesses as having been in the company of Honor. Seven months after the killing, the trial began. Both defendants pleaded not guilty. The taxi driver, a Garda officer, and several of Honor's colleagues testified against them and there was ample compelling evidence. Despite this, the jury deliberated for only three minutes before returning a verdict of not guilty for both men. The case exposed low morals in high places, although it was quickly swept under the carpet and no punishment for the perpetrators was ever forthcoming.

The War on Alcohol

'A pint of plain is your only man.' So said Flann O'Brien in his satirical poem on drinking and its popularity among the people of Ireland. The overconsumption of alcohol was another illicit activity that the government claimed to be keen to stamp out, however. Ireland had no fewer than 3 million people in the Famine era who joined temperance societies and pledged not to imbibe alcohol, but drinking remained a popular, if expensive, pastime nonetheless. In the early days of the new state, poteen, a highly potent but illegal home-made alcohol, was much cheaper to buy than legally produced alternatives. It was especially popular in the economically depressed west of Ireland, where Gardaí conducted hundreds of raids annually to stymie the trade. Several members of independent Ireland's first ever government professed themselves concerned with the drinking culture. Foremost among them was government politician Kevin O'Higgins. O'Higgins had once been an enthusiastic drinker himself but by the 1920s had experienced a 'road to Damascus' conversion. He remarked in 1925 that the poteen trade in the west had led to children 'reeling round the road drunk' on their way to school.

Legal drinking was also considered a problem. Miltown Malbay in Co. Clare may have held the world record for the highest number of pubs per capita in the late nineteenth century when the town had a population of just 1,400, yet boasted thirty-six pubs. Staggering. Things had changed little by 1925, when Ireland had around 13,000 public houses, an average of one pub for every 230 people, a far higher ratio than in England, Scotland or Wales. In response, the government decided to act against the country's widespread alcohol consumption, though they stopped short of implementing prohibition like in the United States. Instead, they introduced strict new laws through the Intoxicating Liquor Act (1924), which aimed to limit alcohol availability. This legislation banned pubs from opening after 10 p.m., restricted alcohol consumption to those over 18, and instituted a 'holy hour' in the middle of the day during which alcohol sales were prohibited. St Patrick's Day and Good Friday were also designated as dry days. On Sundays, meanwhile, a bizarre law decreed that only 'bona fide travellers', or those who lived 3 miles or more from the pub they were in, could be legally served alcohol. Unfortunately, these new restrictions on public houses led to an increased demand for poteen, a drink that was often produced in unsanitary conditions and could cause illness or death.

Despite this high-mindedness, government politicians themselves were not immune to the charms of alcohol and a heavy drinking session may have changed the course of Irish history after the closely contested election of June 1927. A crucial vote on who would form the next government was to be held, and one member rumoured to be voting against the government was John Jinks, a TD for Sligo. Arithmetic seemed to suggest that the government was going to lose by one vote, handing power to Fianna Fáil, who just four years before had been at war with the new state. When the time came to test out the opinions of the politicians, however, Jinks was nowhere to be found. It was later alleged that two government politicians had waylaid Jinks and invited him into a nearby pub, giving him enough intoxicating liquor to persuade him to abandon the idea of going to parliament at all and putting him on a train back to his home county. Jinks later denied this, stating that he abstained for ideological reasons. The government survived with the casting vote of the Ceann Comhairle (Speaker of the House). Jinks was not re-elected to parliament.

Stamping out drinking was a trickier prospect than tackling prostitution and was not a success, although the Legion of Mary led by Frank Duff did their best to deter would-be drinkers. In defence of the LOM, they set up numerous homeless hostels and were compassionate to alcoholics, although this did not win them the praise of committed drinkers. One popular song from 1920s Ireland, called 'Boozing', contained the lyrics:

Now what do the Salvation Army shoot down?
Boozing, bloody well boozing!
And what are they preaching in every town?
Boozing, bloody well boozing!
They preach they don't practise, of that there's no doubt,
And on the street corners, they'll stand and they'll shout,
But what are they doing when the lights have gone out?
Boozing, bloody well boozing!

The War on 'Evil' Literature and Music

Another target of the state's disapproving gaze was 'evil literature'. This could come in the form of newspapers or books that were not seen to be upholding the morality the conservative state was striving for. The Censorship of Publications Board banned more than 12,000 'unwholesome' publications after its foundation in 1929. The novels banned were by both Irish and international authors. Works classified as 'evil' included Brendan Behan's *Borstal Boy*, Edna O'Brien's *Country Girls* and Oscar Wilde's *The Picture of Dorian Gray*.

To modern eyes, the content of these works seems tame, but mentions of contraception, divorce and sex in any form were not deemed appropriate for Irish eyes. Newspapers, particularly English publications such as the *Daily Mail*, were also in the sights of the committee. As early as 1928, a Co. Leitrim priest complained that Ireland was ruined with filthy literature and foreign newspapers. He added that he been in a shop in Dublin and noticed such literature being put into envelopes for remote places all over Ireland. The same priest appears to have been very familiar with the content of such immoral books, although perhaps he had read them only for research purposes.

Oscar Wilde.

It was not just literature that was in the firing line. A fierce, but short-lived, anti-jazz campaign occurred in 1934. Started by another Co. Leitrim priest, a protest was held in the town of Mohill in which 3,000 attendees marched and shouted slogans demanding the banning of jazz music in Ireland and its complete removal from RTÉ, Ireland's only radio station, which had been founded in 1926. The protesters denounced the music genre as communistic and an 'engine of hell'. They also railed against what they called 'jazz dancing', which they believed was a menace to Irish womanhood. The Taoiseach himself, Éamon de Valera, sent a representative to the protest and briefly many newspapers weighed into the campaign, which nevertheless ran out of steam within a short time.

The Fight for Women's Suffrage

The fight for the vote for women goes back well before Irish independence. As early as 1866, 1,500 signatories signed the first suffrage petition presented to Westminster, twenty-five of whom were Irish. Ten years later, Anna and Thomas Haslam established the Dublin Suffrage Association. Incremental progress was made until 1911, when women became eligible to become members of town and county councils. This was four years after similar measures had been adopted in England and there remained vehement opposition to the idea of votes for women in Ireland. After all, Trinity College, Ireland's premier university, had only granted them admission in 1904, despite the first women graduating from an Irish university back in 1884. John Dillon was one of the best-known politicians in Ireland in the First World War era and he would rise to be leader of the Irish Parliamentary Party. He summed up the attitude of many in the establishment when he said: 'Women's Suffrage will,

I believe, be the ruin of our Western civilisation. It will destroy the home, challenging the headship of man, laid down by God. It may come in your time – I hope not in mine!'

Many Irishwomen were undeterred and the tactics to bring attention to their cause grew more radical after 1911. These included heckling politicians' speeches, breaking windows in Dublin Castle and throwing stones at government buildings in the capital. The British Prime Minister, Herbert Asquith, even had an axe thrown at him in July 1912 as he drove through Dublin. Many women were arrested and over two dozen imprisoned for these acts, and some of the prisoners even went on hunger strike in 1913. The First World War brought a split in the suffrage movement, however. Many suffrage societies in England and the north of Ireland suspended their campaign and announced their support of the war effort. Nationalist women refused to countenance this and many joined Cumann na mBan, with Countess Markievicz warning: 'I would ask every nationalist woman to pause before she joined a suffrage society or franchise league that did not include in their programme the freedom of their nation.'[20]

The Easter Rising, in which Cumann na mBan played a crucial role, recognised women and the Proclamation of the Irish Republic specifically included Irish women, a progressive move for the time. Some Irish women got the vote in 1918 and Countess Markievicz, who had fought in the Rising, was the first female elected to Westminster in the same year. Universal franchise was finally extended in 1922, presumably to the ire of John Dillon, although this was hardly the end of the travails of Irish women. In 1937, Éamon de Valera helped to draft a new constitution for the Free State, which was bitterly opposed by many of his former feminist colleagues. A marriage ban lasting

---

20 'Suffrage and the national question', Houses of the Oireachtas, www.oireachtas.ie.

until the 1970s saw women in the public sector being forced to give up their post after their nuptials. The representation of women in Irish politics also moved at a glacial pace for decades, and as late as 1969, there were just three female TDs in the Dáil. A watershed moment came in 1990 when Mary Robinson won the vote to become the seventh president of Ireland, and the first female to hold the role, famously praising the 'women of Ireland, Mná na hÉireann, who instead of rocking the cradle, rocked the system'. In 1997, she was followed into office by Mary McAleese, an advocate for peace in the north of Ireland, making Ireland one of a small number of countries to have had two female heads of state by this time.

Ireland and the Second World War

Ireland had completely different experiences in the First and Second World Wars. The Second World War saw a far smaller number of Irish people choosing to serve, Ireland being decidedly neutral, much to Britain's chagrin. Nevertheless, it quickly became evident that importing goods from Britain or the Continent would soon become difficult or, in some cases, impossible. As a result, rationing of items like clothing, petrol, food and other essentials was deemed necessary and implemented without delay. Ration books were issued to every citizen shortly after the war began, though a thriving black market quickly emerged. Petrol was heavily rationed, leading to significant hardship, with most private vehicles being taken off the roads.

Despite neutrality, some Irishmen and women played a role in the war. Most aided Britain and the Allies, and Cork man James Murphy was one who inadvertently helped their cause. In March 1939, he published the first unedited English translation of Hitler's *Mein Kampf*. This version revealed to English speakers the German leader's intentions to invade Eastern Europe and briefly made Murphy a wanted man in Germany. Emily Anderson also helped the British. The suffragette and professor of languages at University of Galway was a fluent German speaker and she worked in the intelligence division of the British Army. Anderson proved to be an adept codebreaker and was later honoured with an OBE for her contributions. An Irish priest named Monsignor Hugh O'Flaherty saved thousands of lives during the Second World War, hiding both Jews and Allied prisoners of war in Rome.

Another interesting Irish connection was Bridget Hitler, née Dowling, a native of Dublin who married Alois Hitler, the half-brother of the Führer himself, although it is unlikely Adolf Hitler ever set foot on Irish soil. An Irishwoman named Violet Gibson could have changed the course of world history, and maybe even helped to prevent the Second World War, when she attempted to assassinate Benito Mussolini in 1926. The bullet grazed his nose and Il Duce lived to fight another day, and to bring Italy into the most brutal conflict the world has ever known. The devoutly religious Gibson, who had lived in Italy for many years, never fully explained her motivation yet was found guilty but insane, and was detained in an asylum in Italy until her death in 1956.

Ireland did not completely escape the violence of the Second World War and bombs were dropped on Irish soil on several occasions. It is not surprising that the six counties of the north, which remained part of the United Kingdom after partition, were bombed regularly, particularly Belfast, and over 1,000 people were killed in these raids. More surprising was the number of bombs dropped on the neutral Free State. On 26 August 1940, Campile in Co. Wexford was bombed by a single Luftwaffe plane. Three local women were killed. The Shannon family near Kiltealy in Co. Carlow were desperately unlucky when a German bomber flying above released eight bombs that hit their house, destroying the building and killing three members of the family. The North Strand Bombing in Dublin was the deadliest attack, however. Twenty-eight people were killed and hundreds of buildings damaged when, in May 1941, four high-explosive bombs were dropped by the Germans. The Nazis claimed it had been done accidentally, although it may have been a warning to the Irish, who had been covertly helping the Allied cause by providing weather reports and other valuable intelligence. The Irish had also dispatched fire-fighters to aid in combatting fires in the north caused by German bombs, and had secretly released Allied fighters found on their soil. Spy Hermann Görtz, conversely, was taken into custody after he parachuted onto Irish soil and was held for the duration of the war.

The most prominent Irish ally of the Nazis was probably William Joyce. Raised in Galway City, Joyce was known for his intelligence and arrogance. As a teenager, he became hostile to Irish nationalism and befriended British soldiers during the War of Independence. This made him unpopular locally and he fled to England, joined the British Army, and later became involved in the British Union of Fascists. By 1939, as tensions rose between Germany and Britain, Joyce again fled, this time to Germany, where he worked as a radio announcer, gaining fame with his 'Germany Calling' broadcasts. His broadcasts, trumpeting German victories and mocking British leaders, were listened to by millions of Britons, his posh accent earning him the nickname Lord Haw-Haw. After Hitler's death in 1945, Joyce was captured near the German–Danish border, tried for treason by the British, and executed in 1946. His remains were reburied in Galway in 1976. Seán Russell, former chief-of-staff of the IRA, also travelled to Germany and died on board a German submarine after he had met the German foreign minister Joachim von Ribbentrop. In a famous episode deeply resented by the Allies, Taoiseach Éamon de Valera visited the German ambassador to Ireland, Eduard Hempel, on the death of Hitler in 1945. Although de Valera later said this had been a diplomatic courtesy and not out of respect for Hitler, it enraged many in Britain and America.

Strange Scandals in Independent Ireland

There were strange scandals in independent Ireland that seem odd to the modern reader. One bizarre story centred around the appointment of Letitia Dunbar-Harrison to the role of head librarian in Co. Mayo in 1930. The graduate of Modern Literature from Trinity College seemed amply qualified and had won prizes for English. All seemed in order with the appointment until it was discovered by the public at large that she was a member of the Protestant community. Mayo County Council's library committee refused to rubberstamp the appointment, denying that her religion was the cause and claiming that it was a result of her inability to speak Irish. The County Council at large then took the unprecedented step of voting overwhelmingly to reject the successful candidate, something that one local deputy defended by saying, 'The only thing that the Mayo County Council could have been accused of was that they represented the views of 98 per cent of the people of Mayo in this question.' The government dissolved the whole council and replaced it with a commissioner, who immediately confirmed Dunbar-Harrison's appointment. Mayo County Council had many supporters and was backed by the leader of the opposition himself, Éamon de Valera, who stated that libraries were places of education and therefore denominational. Clerical-backed boycotts of the libraries throughout Mayo began after her arrival to the county and thousands of people stayed away from the libraries for one year until Dunbar-Harrison was quietly transferred to a post in the Department of Defence.

Another scandal with religious undertones was the Fethard-on-Sea boycott, which took place in the tiny coastal village in Co. Wexford in 1957. It all started when Fr William Stafford, the local Catholic curate, tried to pressurise Seán Cloney, a Catholic, and his wife Sheila, a Protestant, to send their daughters to the local Catholic school. In response, Sheila decided to leave the parish with the children, travelling to Scotland. Fr Stafford blamed the local Protestant community for her departure, believing she had been aided by them, and he organised a boycott of Protestant-owned businesses in the area. The boycott was strictly adhered to and even the local Catholic schoolteacher was forced to leave her role in the village's tiny Protestant school. The boycott gained international attention and continued for several months until August 1957, when the priest purchased a pack of cigarettes in one of the Protestant-owned shops, indicating that the people had permission to enter them again. Sheila Cloney eventually returned to Fethard-on-Sea, although she did not send her children to the Catholic school. The story was eventually made into a film, *A Love Divided*.

Ireland was certainly a deeply religious place, and it arguably reached the peak of its religiosity in June 1932 when the Eucharistic Congress came to the country. Ireland was chosen to commemorate the 1,500th anniversary of the coming of St Patrick and masses attracting up to a quarter of a million worshippers were held in the Phoenix Park. Half a century later, the moving statues phenomenon of the summer of 1985 also caused a brief stir across Ireland. Reports emerged in several areas nationally of Virgin Mary statues moving inexplicably. Thousands of people gathered at grottos, hoping to witness the statues physically move, and there were also claims of spoken messages and apparitions of the Blessed Virgin. This short-lived religious fervour tapered off quickly, although pilgrims still come to see the statue at Ballinspittle, Co. Cork, where the phenomenon began.

The 'Battle of Baltinglass' was another bizarre local feud that came to national prominence. Baltinglass is a small town in west Wicklow and it seemed an unlikely place for a national flashpoint concerning the government and the corruption with which jobs were given out, but this was how it transpired. In this case, in 1950, a local woman named Helen Cooke was considered a shoo-in for the job of local sub-postmaster, a much sought after position in rural Ireland at the time. The job came with reasonable pay and prestige in an era when the country was in a perilous economic state. Cooke had been in the position in an interim fashion for several years and was confident of the appointment. Unfortunately for her, the Fine Gael-led government of the day saw things differently and gave the job to a supporter of the government, Michael Farrell. The local community was incensed at what many saw as blatant jobbery and Cooke herself was not willing to take it lying down. A campaign against the decision began. Telephone poles were cut down, while communication cables were severed. Pickets were held at the post office and outside the Dáil, and Cooke even set up a rival post office. The story grabbed international headlines, with journalists from all over the world descending on the small town to write about the bizarre feud, which ended after a month with Farrell resigning, the government being toppled and Cooke being reinstated in her post.

It was not the last time an Irish government would fall on a seemingly trivial matter. The 1982 budget failed for several reasons, principally a value-added tax on children's shoes and a couple of pence on the price of a pint. This led to the collapse of the government. Six years earlier, in October 1976, the president of Ireland, Cearbhall Ó Dálaigh, resigned after being called 'a thundering disgrace' by the Minister for Defence, Paddy Donegan, when Donegan addressed Irish soldiers in Mullingar. Donegan's unprecedented attack was directed at the president due to the latter's referral of the government's controversial anti-terrorism legislation to the Supreme Court to judge its constitutionality. Ó Dálaigh resigned within days, amidst rumours that a stronger and more profane word than 'disgrace' was used by Donegan.

Northern Ireland

Northern Ireland, or the six counties of Antrim, Armagh, Fermanagh, Tyrone, Derry and Down, came into being in 1920. Fermanagh and Tyrone were evenly divided between unionists, who were generally Protestant and loyal to the United Kingdom, and nationalists, who viewed themselves as Irish and were usually Catholic. The four other counties had clear unionist majorities, leading the unionist authorities to conclude that they had a safe margin to ensure a unionist majority for centuries to come. The state was born with violence, particularly in Belfast, most areas of which became balkanised, many either almost 100 per cent Catholic or 100 per cent Protestant. The state continued to be ruled by 'A Protestant parliament for a Protestant people' as James Craig, the north's first Prime Minister, described it, but an uneasy peace was occasionally broken by spells of violence between the communities.

The Troubles, which erupted in the north in the dying days of the 1960s and continued until the Good Friday Agreement in 1998, were a result of this sharp religious and political divide. The perception among Catholics was that unionists, who made up some 65 per cent of the population of the north at the outset of the Troubles, were given plum government jobs and better access to housing. This perception was grounded in reality and electoral areas were also gerrymandered at times in the north, the boundaries drawn in such a way as to benefit unionists. In Co. Fermanagh, in the early days of Northern Ireland, the majority Catholic population regularly saw two out of three seats being filled by unionists, for example. The Troubles were preceded by a civil rights association using tactics like those seen in the rights movement of African-Americans in the 1960s, but paramilitaries from both sides stepped into the fragmented society and countless numbers of bombings and shootings would lead to some 3,500 deaths between 1969 and 1998.

Even Irish politicians became involved – the Arms Crisis occurred in 1970, when the then Minister for Finance, Charles Haughey, was accused of engaging in a conspiracy to import arms for republican use in the north of Ireland. Despite the terrible violence and bloodshed that plagued the area from the late 1960s until well into the 1990s, many wished for permanent peace and several people from the north of Ireland won the Nobel Peace Prize. Mairéad Maguire and Betty Williams, two women from either side of the religious divide, were co-recipients of the 1976 Nobel Prize after their peace activism in the height of the Troubles, while politicians John Hume and David Trimble, a nationalist and a unionist respectively, received the same prize in 1998 after they helped to get the Good Friday Agreement across the line. Today, Northern Ireland is unrecognisable. It welcomes hundreds of thousands of tourists yearly to see the Titanic Museum, the Giant's Causeway or the areas where the popular television series *Game of Thrones* was filmed.

The society is now close to an even divide in terms of demographics, although religious beliefs have moderated and sectarian divisions have cooled. However, many 'Peace Walls' remain in place, dividing the two communities in urban areas, most notably between the Falls and Shankill Roads in West Belfast. They are a reminder of the sharp societal divisions over whether Northern Ireland should unite with the south or stay as part of the United Kingdom, a question that is likely to occupy the minds of people and politicians for the foreseeable future.

The Celtic Tiger

Much of the lost decades of the 1970s and '80s in Ireland, when large proportions of the country's young people left their homeland out of economic necessity, occurred while Charles Haughey was Taoiseach or Minister for Finance. Haughey grimly warned the country that they were living way beyond their means in preparing them for an austerity budget in 1980. It would later transpire that Haughey was no stranger to the high life himself and owned a private island, Inishvickillane off Co. Kerry, as well as a yacht and substantial property assets. These decades of economic stagnation were followed by a foreign direct-investment-fuelled boom in the 1990s and 2000s that led to many of the world's biggest pharmaceutical and IT companies setting up in Ireland, causing incredible economic growth that came to be known as the Celtic Tiger.

The period was renowned for its free spending, and there were many who felt the government lost the run of itself. One famous incident occurred on *The Late Late Show* in 1999 when Irish MEP Pádraig Flynn was asked by a journalist about his pay and expenses. Flynn admitted that he earned approximately £100,000 after tax, adding that he needed to 'run a home in Dublin, Castlebar and Brussels. I wanna tell you something, try it sometime, when you have a couple of cars and three houses and three homes and a few housekeepers.' This left the audience incredulous, most undoubtedly feeling that they would never have an opportunity to try it sometime. Meanwhile, the price of houses rose in response to the rise in wages and, by the 2000s, dissenting voices were beginning to think that this had all the signs of a property bubble. The Taoiseach of Ireland disagreed. Bertie Ahern famously said he did not understand these people: 'Sitting on the sides cribbing and moaning is a lost opportunity. I don't know how people who engage in that don't commit suicide.'[21]

He also boasted that, 'The boom is getting boomier.' This same Bertie Ahern was the Irish Minister for Finance who did not have a bank account. Interviewed about his financial dealings in the Mahon Tribunal, Ahern told his interrogators that although he had been Minister for Finance in the late 1980s and early 1990s, he did not in fact have a bank account and dealt exclusively with cash. When questioned about the large amounts of cash he was known to have spent, he explained that a portion of it came from a win on the horses, while some of the rest was 'a whip-around' from close friends. As the Celtic Tiger teetered on the brink in 2007, government politicians insisted that a soft landing was imminent, rather than an economic bust. Sadly, September 2008 brought just such a bust globally and Irish banks would soon feel the effects of a recession that lasted close to a decade. House prices would plummet, the economy would haemorrhage jobs and the Celtic Tiger would become a distant memory.

---

21 *Irish Independent*, 5 July 2007.

10

Other Odd Aspects of Ireland

Strange Religious Happenings in Ireland

Irishman Oliver Plunkett was the last Catholic executed for his faith in England. Born in Loughcrew, Co. Meath, in the seventeenth century, Plunkett received his education in Rome, where he studied for the priesthood. He stayed in Italy for some two decades until he was appointed Archbishop of Armagh. The Irish Catholic Church was in a poor state but he succeeded in reorganising it, confirming tens of thousands of people and founding a successful Catholic school. With persecution against Catholics by the authorities worsening, Plunkett became a wanted man and was arrested for treason, being falsely accused of facilitating a French invasion. In the knowledge that he was unlikely to be convicted by an Irish jury, Plunkett was instead tried in England and found guilty. He was hanged, drawn and quartered in 1681. He was canonised in 1975 and is now the Patron Saint of Peace and Reconciliation. Since the 1920s, his head has been on display in a gilded case in St Peter's Church, Drogheda, Co. Louth.

Plunkett was not the first high-ranking Irish clergyman to be executed. The Bishop of Down and Connor, Conor O'Devany, had also been hanged, drawn and quartered in 1612 for allegedly assisting in rebellion against the Crown. Plunkett would not be the last man of the cloth executed, either. Fr Nicholas Sheehy was the parish priest of the small Tipperary village of Clogheen. He had been an advocate for tenants' rights and a fierce opponent of the Penal Laws, and was thus considered an enemy of the Crown. For this reason, he was arrested for inciting rebellion. Found not guilty, he was re-arrested on a spurious charge of the murder of a man named John Bridge in 1764. Despite having a credible alibi, Fr Sheehy was found guilty and hanged on 15 March 1766 outside the County Gaol in Clonmel, Co. Tipperary.

Catholics were not the only victims of persecution, as a localised campaign against the Jewish people of Limerick showed in 1904. It was led by a local priest, Fr John Creagh, who claimed that Jews in the local business community had caused 'their rags to be exchanged for silks' by exploiting their customers. A boycott of sorts occurred and there were several incidents of intimidation, boycotting and vandalism. Some Irish politicians, such as Michael Davitt, publicly opposed the boycott. Others, including Arthur Griffith, supported it. Eventually, many of the city's small Jewish community left the city and moved away permanently. Some went abroad, while others relocated to Cork. The son of one of their number, Gerald Goldberg, rose to the position of Lord Mayor of Cork. Members of the Jewish faith have otherwise had a mostly long and harmonious life in Ireland. William Annyas was a Jewish mayor of the town of Youghal, Co. Cork, as early as 1555. Robert Briscoe, an Orthodox Jew of Lithuanian heritage, is probably the highest-profile follower of Judaism in Irish history, however. He was an IRA volunteer in the War of Independence and later served as a TD for Fianna Fáil for close to four decades, also holding the position of Lord Mayor of Dublin twice in the 1950s and '60s.

Transport

Ireland has had roads since time immemorial. The annals of the Four Masters speak of five ancient highways that led to Tara, Co. Meath, the seat of the kings. For centuries afterwards, the roads of Ireland were little more than bridle paths, but an Italian entrepreneur named Charles Bianconi revolutionised Irish transport and the construction of better-quality roads followed. Beginning in 1815, Bianconi slowly began to build a system of horse-drawn carriages to create an extensive network of affordable, timetabled routes that ultimately spanned most of the country, from Belfast to Cork. These jaunting cars could accommodate six passengers. In the early days, many believed the business was destined to fail and Bianconi secretly launched a second jaunting car on the same route using an alias, creating competition for his own operation and drumming up interest in the venture. Bianconi's service would eventually encompass some 100 cars and drivers and 140 stations, offering reliable transportation between the major towns and cities. Railways began to make inroads eventually, but Bianconi cleverly changed his timetable so that he could pick up passengers from stations and drop them at their ultimate destination.

The first railway in Irish history was opened in 1834 between Dublin and Monkstown. It was extended to the wealthy seaside suburb and port of Kingstown, later named Dún Laoghaire, in 1837 and by the 1850s it ran all the way to Bray, Co. Wicklow. It proved enormously popular, serving commuters and day trippers alike. Many other railways were constructed in the following decades but none were as unique as the Lartigue Railway, which opened in 1888 and ran the 10 miles between Listowel and the seaside resort of Ballybunion in Co. Kerry. The monorail-type train was the only one of its type in the world and was considered a marvel of the ages. Further railways continued to open throughout the nineteenth century, and by the 1920s Ireland had an extensive network of around 3,500 miles with tracks in every county. Not everyone was impressed with the service offered. Percy French, who wrote many songs that lampooned aspects of Irish society of the day, famously composed the song 'Are Ye Right There Michael?' This made fun of the notoriously slow West Clare Railway and was written after French had a terrible experience on the train in 1896 when he was inconvenienced by a five-hour delay, causing him to miss a concert he was due to give. French sued the West Clare Railway Company for loss of earnings. Legend has it that French arrived late for the court case, quipping to the judge, 'I am sorry, Your Honour, I came by the West Clare Railway!' He was awarded £10.

With the growing popularity of the motor car, railways came under threat and many rural lines were closed. Galway to Clifden, the last line to open in 1895, was also the first to close in 1935 and many others would follow suit over the next three decades. In the modern day, the railway network in Ireland connects little more than the major cities on the island. Large counties such as Donegal have no train services at all, although the mode of transport is experiencing something of a resurgence with a trickle of lines opening and reopening since 2000. The Luas also opened in Dublin in 2004, the first tram in the capital for over half a century. It has been an enormous success, attracting close to 50 million passengers a year.

The motor car has a storied history in Ireland too, and the world's first road fatality was likely to have occurred here in 1869 when the 42-year-old acclaimed scientist Mary Ward died after she fell under the wheels of a moving vehicle she had been travelling in near the town of Birr, Co. Offaly. The vehicle was not a motor car as we know it today. It was described in newspapers as a 'road locomotive steam-engine', and Ward was killed when it went around a sharp corner in the town, causing her to fall from the vehicle, which then drove over her. She died instantly.

Meanwhile, the first motor car as we recognise them today to make its way to Ireland was said have been a Serpollet model, imported in 1896. Numbers would increase exponentially year on year. In 1915, there were just under 10,000 cars in Ireland, with a similar number of motorcycles. A century later, there were some 2 million cars in the republic alone, while the number of motorcycles had increased much more slowly, to just over 35,000. This has led to many improvements in people's lifestyles, but there have also been tragedies. In 1972, there were an incredible 640 deaths on Irish roads, the worst year on record. This number has declined steadily since, with the introduction of seat belts, more rigorous testing of drivers and cars and strict drink-driving laws. Road deaths now average about 170 a year, making the country far safer for motorists than the European Union average. This comes in at 3.4 deaths per 100,000 people on Ireland's extensive road network of some 62,000 miles.

This road network has improved markedly since the turn of the twentieth century. Construction on the first dual carriageway in Ireland was started in 1938 near Belfast, although in the south such a road would not be constructed until 1968, when the Dublin to Naas Dual Carriageway was opened. Several motorways have been built since this time. The M1 goes from Dublin due north to Belfast, the M2 north-west in the direction of Derry and so on in a radial fashion, until the M11, which goes due south from the capital to Wexford. The construction of these motorways has generally been welcomed but they have not always been without controversy. The M3 motorway passes near the sacred Hill of Tara, something that caused huge controversy during its construction. Tara's sacred status has endured since it was the destination of all main Irish routes in ancient times and it has been closely guarded by the Irish people. In 1899, members of the British-Israel Association of London arrived in Tara. Their plan was to excavate the sacred hill, a place where they believed they were likely to find the Ark of the Covenant, a chest said to hold the stone tablets inscribed with the Ten Commandments. Their actions caused uproar and luminaries of Irish cultural life such as Maud Gonne, William Butler Yeats and Douglas Hyde protested at the site, singing nationalist songs and lighting bonfires. The Irish press backed the protesters and the would-be archaeologists were eventually forced to move on.

In terms of aviation, the first flight in Ireland occurred in 1909, six years after the Wright Brothers of North Carolina became the first aviators in the world. The mastermind was car mechanic Harry Ferguson of Co. Down, who designed and built his own plane that, after a few failed attempts, flew for 160 yards. Ferguson went on to develop the three-point linkage system for tractors, an innovation that revolutionised agriculture forever. He also became a major player in the Massey Ferguson company, renowned globally for its agricultural machinery to this day. Henry Ford, with whom Ferguson had a fruitful partnership, was the inventor of the Model T car and a man who made the ownership of a motor vehicle an achievable dream for the ordinary family. He had strong Irish roots, his father having been born in a labourer's cottage in Co. Cork. Ford did not forget his heritage and invested heavily in Cork, building a Ford plant in the city that began by manufacturing tractors and then progressed to building cars. At its height, it employed 7,000 workers, making it by far the largest employer in Ireland.

Henry Ford. (Library of Congress)

Irish Place Names

Irish place names generally come from the Irish language, but most were replaced by a meaningless phonetic name to make them easier to pronounce in the English language. Most counties follow this rule: Ciarraí, for example, means 'tribe of Ciar'. It was anglicised as Kerry. Cork, or Corcaigh, probably comes from the Irish word corcach, 'a marshy place'. In some cases, however, places have retained the translation the Vikings placed on them centuries ago. Cill Mhantáin, which translates as 'church of the toothless one', became Wicklow in old Norse, possibly from Víkingr-ló, 'Viking meadow'. The county retains the name in its English language form to this day. In a small number of cases, the name given to a town or village in English bore no relation at all to the Irish name that had preceded it by centuries. Virginia, a town in Co. Cavan, is one example, its original name being Achadh an Iúir, meaning the field of the yew tree. Another example is Miltown Malbay in Co. Clare, the Irish language version of which is Sráid na Cathrach (street of the ringfort).

The longest place name in Ireland is 'Muckanaghederdauhaulia', or 'Muiceanach idir Dhá Sháile' in Irish. It is near the village of Rosmuck in Co. Galway and translates as 'pig-shaped ridge between two salt waters'. The shortest place name is probably (Lough) Ta, all Irish lakes having lough before their name, giving this just a two-letter moniker. Unusual place names in Ireland include Hackballscross, Co. Louth; Nobber, Co. Meath; Dung, Co. Cavan; and Bastardstown, Co. Wexford. If the former two reverted to their original Irish names of Crois an Mhaoir and An Obair it may be preferable. In the latter two cases, Dung has the same name in Irish as it does in English, while Baile Bhastaird may not be much of an improvement.

Place names in Ireland are not always without controversy. The most prominent example is Derry/Londonderry, the former ancient name, coming from the Irish word 'Doire' meaning 'oak', being generally favoured by nationalists, with unionists often using the latter name, which was given to the city by the British government in the seventeenth century after an influx of English planters, many from London. In the years around Irish independence, several place names that had connections with Ireland's former colonial masters in Britain were changed to a more Irish-sounding name. Several of these were done before independence was even secured. Prominent among them was Kingstown in Co. Dublin, which had been called Dunleary in earlier centuries but was given the royal-sounding name in 1821 following the visit of King George IV. It reverted to Dún Laoghaire in 1920. Queenstown in Cork, the foremost port in Ireland at the time, was renamed Cóbh in the same year.

Other examples were Queen's County and King's County, which reverted to their older names, Laois and Offaly respectively. Maryborough, the county town of Laois, was renamed Portlaoise,

Cobh, formerly Queenstown, Co. Cork. (Library of Congress)

and Parsonstown and Phillipstown in Co. Offaly became Birr and Daingean respectively. In the latter case, Phillipstown was named after a Spanish king. This did not save its moniker, however, and it was given the more Irish-sounding name in 1922. There are other examples all over the country: Kingwilliamstown in Co. Cork being renamed Ballydesmond is just one. This did not happen in every case – other towns with unmistakably English names, such as Manorhamilton in Co. Leitrim (Cluainín, or little meadow, in Irish), retained their names.

It was not just towns and villages that received this treatment. Many railway stations would come to be named after Irish patriots, particularly leaders of the 1916 Rising. One of Ireland's most important transport links, Kingsbridge Station, was renamed Heuston Station in 1966, the fiftieth anniversary of the Easter Rising, after Seán Heuston, an executed rebel and himself a former railway worker. Main streets in towns and cities all over the country were also regularly given a new moniker in honour of Irish heroes. There are at least thirteen Pearse Streets in Ireland, for example, named after Patrick Pearse, while Ireland's main thoroughfare, the grand Sackville Street through Dublin city centre, became O'Connell Street in honour of the Liberator himself. A 40ft statue of Daniel O'Connell now stands on the street and although loyalists attempted to blow it up in 1971, the damage was minimal.

Some British-era statues did not do well out of Irish independence either. On 25 May 1922, a statue of Lord Dunkellin, a former Galway MP, British Army captain and staunch supporter of the British Empire, was torn down in the city's main square. After standing for fifty years, the monument was unceremoniously hauled through the streets by crowds and dumped into the sea at the nearby Spanish Arch. A statue of loyalist icon King William of Orange that had sat on College Green in Dublin City since 1701 was also blown up, on Armistice Day, 11 November 1928. It was later replaced by a statue to Thomas Davis. Nelson's Pillar, built in honour of British Admiral Horatio Nelson, was also blown up by the IRA in Dublin in 1966. The Spire was afterwards built on the spot. It is a deeply divisive 393ft pole reaching skywards that has derisively been nicknamed 'the stiletto in the ghetto'. Not all British-era monuments fared so badly. The Wellington Obelisk, standing at over 200ft in the Phoenix Park, remains in situ 200 years after its construction.

Irish Cities

Ireland has several recognised cities. The most well-known of these is the capital, Dublin. Others include Cork, Limerick, Galway and Waterford in the south, and Belfast and Derry in the north. Surprisingly, Belfast, the second largest city on the island of Ireland, only received its city charter in 1888. There is some confusion over whether Sligo qualifies as a city or not, although many of its denizens certainly believe that it should. There are several other official cities, however; in Northern Ireland, since the 1990s, Lisburn, Newry and Bangor have all been conferred with city status, despite their relatively small size. Kilkenny has also been in possession of a royal charter since 1383, which allows it to be designated as a city despite being far smaller than many Irish towns. It was even the Irish capital at one stage. The ecclesiastically important settlement of Armagh has likewise been long-conferred with city status, despite being home to fewer than 20,000 people. Interestingly, Cashel in Co. Tipperary was also once considered a city, as was Clogher in Co. Tyrone, a small village today. Downpatrick, Co. Down, reputed to be the resting place of Ireland's three foremost saints, Patrick, Bridget and Colmcille, also once had the right to be called a city. There are a number of large towns in Ireland clamouring for city status today. These include Ballymena in the north and Drogheda and Tallaght in the south.

Irish Islands

Ireland is home to hundreds of islands, most of them uninhabited. Many of these have an important place in Irish history – Fastnet Rock barely qualifies as an island, but is Ireland's southernmost point and is known as the 'Teardrop of Ireland' as it was the last part of the island many emigrants from the country would see before their departure, many never to return. The island population in Ireland has decreased markedly over the last two centuries. From over 200 populated islands before the Famine, there were just 61 in 1991, a number that has decreased further since that time. Barely ten offshore islands have populations exceeding 100 people today. Inishmore, the largest of the Aran Islands, has the highest population of any offshore island, numbering slightly over 800, down from over 2,500 before the Famine. Other islands have suffered catastrophic drops in population in the same time frame. Bere Island off Co. Cork had over 2,100 inhabitants in 1841, a number that has plummeted to a little over 200 today, barely 10 per cent of its former population.

Many Irish islands have also been bridged, most at the latter end of the nineteenth century. Ireland's largest island, Achill off Co. Mayo, is one example. Dursey Island off Co. Cork has no bridge but is instead connected to the mainland by Ireland's only cable car, although it has no year-round residents. This is reputed to be the only cable car in Europe to cross open sea. Many other Irish islands are tidal, such as Coney Island in Co. Sligo, which some believe gave its name to the American island of the same name.

Many islands are hugely popular with tourists and each has a unique history and cultural life. The now uninhabited Scattery Island in Co. Clare is famous for its well-preserved monastery, for example, while Tory Island off Donegal, the most remote inhabited place in Ireland, situated 8 miles off the coast, elects

Scattery Island, off Co. Clare. (Charles Johnston, *Ireland: Historic and Picturesque*, 1902)

its own king to rule over its 140 residents. Dublin's Lambay Island has a colony of over 100 wallabies, introduced there in the 1950s. Meanwhile, Garinish Island off Co. Cork is famous for its picturesque walled gardens and was also once a haven for famous writers, welcoming Agatha Christie and George Bernard Shaw, who came here in the early 1920s while writing his play *Saint Joan*. The Blasket Islands surely have the greatest legacy in literature, however. In the decades before their depopulation in 1954, the isolated islands off the Kerry coast, with a population of barely fifty people, produced no fewer than six authors of renown, most notably Peig Sayers, whose work was studied by Irish secondary school students for decades.

The furthest outpost of Ireland is Rockall, less an island than an uninhabitable rock, over 200 miles off the coast of Donegal in the North Atlantic Ocean. The rock is the only piece of land in a vast maritime area, which gives it strategic importance, and there remains a relatively good-natured dispute between Ireland, Iceland and the United Kingdon as to which country has sovereignty over it. Even Denmark has thrown its hat into the ring as the outcrop's rightful owner. The patriotic Irish folk band the Wolfe Tones even released a song in the 1970s called 'Rock on Rockall' that announced its opposition to British claims over the remote and uninhabitable rocky islet in the North Atlantic!

Irish Names

The most common Irish surnames have changed little in the last century. According to the 1901 census, the ten most common surnames on the island (and the numbers of people with those names) were:

1. Murphy (56,648)
2. Kelly (46,480)
3. Walsh (35,358)
4. Ryan (30,795)
5. Sullivan (30,239)
6. Byrne (28,224)
7. Doyle (20,636)
8. Reilly (19,682)
9. Gallagher (19,599)
10. Lynch (18,121)

All of these surnames remain common today, with the top five in modern Ireland comprising Murphy, Kelly, Byrne, O'Brien and Walsh, indicating that O'Brien has risen well up the ranks, with little change otherwise.

First names are a different matter and these have transformed completely in the last century. Among men, in 1901, the ten most common names, in order, were:

John, Patrick, James, Michael, Thomas, William, Joseph, Edward, Daniel and Peter.

For babies born today, conversely, the most common names for boys are: Jack, Noah, Rian, Cillian, James, Tadhg, Fionn, Liam,

Oisin and Charlie. Only the name James remains from over a century ago and there are now six names whose origin comes from the Irish language, compared with zero in 1901.

For women, meanwhile, the most popular names in 1901 were:

Mary, Bridget, Margaret, Ellen, Catherine, Kate, Annie, Anne, Elizabeth and Maggie.[22]

The most recent statistics today indicate the popularity of Sophie, Éabha, Grace, Emily, Fiadh, Lily, Olivia, Amelia, Sadie and Mia. In this list, there are two names, Éabha and Fiadh, originating from the Irish language and no names at all remaining from 1901.

Irish Time and Money

For many thousands of years Irish people were mainly self-sufficient and bought very little. When they needed something, they generally bartered with each other or perhaps took the desired item by force. Cows were among the foremost symbols of wealth in Celtic times. The earliest Irish coins were silver pennies, thought to have been minted by the Vikings around AD 1000. These coins were used for trade among themselves and with Vikings from other regions. The Irish word for penny, pingin, comes from an old Viking term. In the fifteenth century, Ireland was granted its own distinct currency by the English, which remained in use for about 200 years, although, at that time, money was almost exclusively used by the upper classes. The Bank of Ireland was established in 1783, but by 1826 Ireland

22 CSO Census of Ireland, 1901.

was no longer allowed to mint its own coins and instead used British currency. This remained the case until Ireland gained independence in 1922.

In the initial years of independence, the money used in Ireland was the same as that of Britain. Ireland finally took the plunge in 1928 and introduced its own coinage, ridding itself of the money with royal insignia that had been used until then. There was, of course, huge debate over what the various coins should depict. Ireland remained deeply divided after the civil war and one man's hero was another's bitter foe. W.B. Yeats was a prominent member of the designing committee and he helped to come up with the novel idea that native Irish animals should be depicted rather than people. A horse, a bull, a wolfhound, a hare and a salmon were among the animals chosen for the coins, then shillings, crowns and so on. There was a harp on the other side of each coin. This choice of animals proved popular and was considered a trait largely unique to Irish currency. Banknotes did feature people, and over the years these included James Joyce, Daniel O'Connell, Queen Medb and Douglas Hyde.

On Decimal Day, Monday, 15 February 1971, Ireland finally decimalised its currency, meaning that a pound was now worth 100 pennies rather than 240. They also began to phase out several beloved coins, including the halfpenny, which was withdrawn in 1986. Ireland used this new decimalised currency, the punt, until 2002, when it joined a currency union and adopted the Euro, which remains in use to this day. Ireland gradually adopted the metric system in all aspects from the 1970s onwards, with kilometres replacing miles on road signs a prominent example, although a pint retained its original name as ordering 568 millilitres of beer was not considered to have the same ring to it.

In earlier years, Ireland had not followed the British in everything they did and there were many units of measurement peculiar to the island. Among them was the Irish mile, which was slightly longer than its British equivalent. There was also an Irish acre and Dublin Mean Time, which was some twenty-five minutes behind its London counterpart until they were standardised in 1916. The Republic of Ireland and Northern Ireland even had two different times during the Second World War, when Britain set its clocks two hours ahead of Greenwich Mean Time to preserve fuel and Ireland did not follow suit. This situation continued until the war's end, with locals joking that you could leave Dundalk in Co. Louth and arrive in Newry, Co. Down, 16 miles away, before you left! Ireland also used the Julian Calendar in earlier centuries, meaning that the dates we ascribe to various pivotal events are often incorrect. The Battle of the Boyne, for example, commemorated each 12 July, actually occurred on 1 July according to the Julian Calendar in use at the time. Ireland only began to utilise the Gregorian calendar in 1752.

Strange Facts of Irish Weather and Natural Life

Ireland has a temperate climate, although it is a country synonymous with large amounts of rain. Nevertheless, like many countries, it has known its fair share of unusual and extreme weather. One event that is unparalleled in recent Irish history is the phenomenon known as the Great Lisbon Earthquake, by some accounts measuring 9 on the Richter Scale, which occurred on 1 November 1755 and caused huge loss of life in Portugal. It also created a tremendous tsunami, which struck the south coast of Ireland three hours afterwards. Towns such as Kinsale in Co. Cork suffered enormous damage, with widespread flooding occurring and boats being torn from their moorings. The tsunami also travelled further up the coast, destroying much of the Spanish Arch in Galway City. The outline of the southern coast of Ireland may even have been altered in places due to the ferocity of the waves.

It is impossible to know how many deaths, or how much damage to property, occurred in Ireland in the aftermath of this earthquake, but it is believed that the huge swells resulting from the earthquake reached as far as the Caribbean Sea.

The Year without a Summer, as 1816 was called, was another freak occurrence that caused great hardship. The eruption of Mount Tambora in Indonesia the previous year had spat huge amounts of dust into the sky, changing climate patterns and causing Europe to suffer its coldest summer on record, resulting in widespread crop failures and major food shortages. The reason for this weather was not understood at the time and many put it down to divine unhappiness with the state of the world. Famine was the inevitable result of the poor weather in Ireland and crop growth was exceptionally poor. Deaths mounted as the year went on and multiple food riots were instigated by the desperate people in towns and cities around the country. Thankfully, 1817 would largely see a return to normal conditions.

Another infamous event was the Night of the Big Wind, or Oíche na Gaoithe Mhóire as it was known to Irish speakers. It was likely the most catastrophic natural event in modern Irish history. On 4 January 1839, heavy snow fell, but the following morning brought an unusually mild and sunny day. In the afternoon, an eerie calm settled over the land, with a stillness in the air and not a breath of wind, which many found unsettling. By 3 p.m., light rain began to fall, and shortly afterwards a rumble from the Atlantic Ocean could be heard on the west coast. The wind picked up sharply, though it did not seem particularly out of the ordinary for a west of Ireland winter. However, within hours the wind's intensity grew, and by 10 p.m. Ireland was struck by a violent hurricane that raged until the next morning. As the wind howled, most people huddled in their homes, praying for the storm to end. The state of homes in pre-Famine Ireland was shockingly poor, with many being thatched and constructed from perishable materials.

The damage was immense. Across the country, thousands of chimneys collapsed, roofs were torn off houses, countless trees fell onto buildings, and an unknown number of fires broke out in homes, often sparked by embers from hearths landing on thatched roofs. The following morning revealed scenes of complete devastation, and newspapers swiftly began reporting on the widespread destruction. Dozens of ships were sunk and many sailors lost their lives. There were many miraculous escapes also:

> We may mention a poor woman named Tunney, and eight children, upon whom the roof first fell in, and before they could extricate themselves, the partition wall came thundering down over the already fallen rafters and thatch. They were all dragged out from beneath the ruins, happy to say, unhurt.[23]

Ireland does occasionally get hot weather and dry periods. It was stated in 1765 that the River Shannon had run dry due to a prolonged drought and people were able to walk across it. The hottest ever Irish temperature, 33.3° Celsius (92°F), was recorded at Kilkenny Castle on 26 June 1887, although at that time Ireland used the Fahrenheit scale to measure temperature. In recent years, 1995 was among the most memorable summers, with Kilkenny having twenty-seven days with temperatures exceeding 25°. In many years, this might occur on as little as two or three days. In 2020, the year remembered for the beginnings of Covid-19 lockdowns, there were months of fine weather in the early days of the pandemic.

The coldest temperature ever recorded in Ireland was at Markree Castle, Co. Sligo, in January 1881, when it was an Arctic -19.1°C (-2°F). Another notably cold period in Ireland occurred between January and March 1947, when temperatures dropped to -14° in parts and did not exceed zero on many days. There were also regular

---

23 *Connaught Telegraph*, 9 January 1839.

Kilkenny Castle, site of Ireland's hottest recorded temperature. (Photograph by the author)

fierce blizzards. The early months of 1963 are also remembered for how bitterly cold they were, as were the winters of both 2009 and 2010. These are, of course, only since records began. Anecdotal evidence suggests icebergs appeared off the Irish coast in the winter of 1740, a time of extreme cold that froze animals and crops in the fields, leading to a terrible famine in Ireland that probably killed up to one-eighth of the population. In Irish, this year was referred to as Bliain an Áir (the Year of the Slaughter).

Interestingly, there are major differences in the climate of different parts of our small island. Counties such as Wexford and Carlow are known as the sunny south-east due to the amount of sunshine they get, while mountainous areas in the west are far wetter. Kerry is often recorded as the wettest county. Villages such as Leenane, Co. Galway, and Newport, Co. Mayo, have also in various years won the not-sought-after crown of the wettest places in Ireland, with over 300 days featuring rain not unheard of. Rain of a different kind occurred in Castlecomer, Co. Kilkenny, on 30 April 1887 when a thick black liquid fell from the sky and continued for some time, giving local wells a black colour and rendering water undrinkable. The cause of this bizarre phenomenon led to much debate, but the most likely explanation centres around Castlecomer being a coal-mining area and an earlier storm having lifted coal dust into the sky that later fell in the rain. Stranger still was an occurrence in the summer of 1928 when dozens of small red-coloured fish fell on to the farm of James McMaster in Drumhirk, Co. Down, an inland area some miles from Strangford Lough. No answer as to why this occurred could be found in the newspapers of the day, but it was reported on as far away as Australia. Even the northern lights can occasionally be seen in Ireland, particularly in the north around Co. Donegal, when climactic conditions are agreeable. The aurora borealis is also more likely to be seen in Ireland's 'dark-sky reserves', areas with low populations and tiny levels of light pollution. These can be found in the mountains of south Co. Kerry, the Nephin Beg Range in Co. Mayo and the Om Dark Sky Park in the Sperrin Mountains in Co. Derry.

Strange tales of Irish Animals, Plants and Nature

As regards native mammals, Ireland has fewer than many other European countries due to its isolation from the continent. Commonly seen animals do include hedgehogs, badgers, foxes and otters, the latter usually spotted along water courses. Ireland is home to six national parks where other mammals will also be seen regularly, particularly deer, pine martens and hares. These are: Wicklow Mountains, the largest national park, covering 205 sq km; Wild Nephin; Glenveagh; Killarney; The Burren; and Connemara National Park.

Some animals that are common in Ireland today are not in fact native but were introduced by humans. These include rats, rabbits and grey squirrels, although all have been in Ireland long enough to be completely unremarkable. Rabbits are in fact native to south-west Europe and north Africa, and were only introduced to Ireland by the Normans in the twelfth century as they were valued for their meat and fur. In the case of the grey squirrel, however, it has damaged the habitat of the smaller native red squirrel. The grey squirrels are larger and stockier than their red equivalent and appear to descend from several grey squirrels that ended up in the midlands of Ireland in the early twentieth century, having being brought here from North America. The grey squirrel has begun to dominate the east of the country, although conservation work has seen a resurgence in the numbers of red squirrels in recent years.

There are many surprising animals that were at one time resident in Ireland. These include elk, reindeer and brown bears. Reindeer fossil bones predating the Ice Age were found in caves

Connemara National Park. (Photograph by the author)

in several counties in the late nineteenth and early twentieth century, but they may have died out due to the warming climate after the Ice Age, which depleted lichens and other food sources on which they relied. The bones of a brown bear can also be seen in Aillwee Cave in Co. Clare, although they have been extinct in Ireland for well over 2,000 years. Wolves were great in number in relatively recent history, as James Hardiman recounted in 1820:

> After the wars of 1641, the ravages of the wolves were so great throughout Ireland, as to excite the attention of the state wolf hunters who were appointed in various districts who helped to rid the country of these ferocious animals.[24]

Indeed, governments both before and after this point paid a bounty for any dead wolf. Forestry cover in Ireland had also dwindled by the seventeenth century, depriving the wolf of its natural habitat. The last wild Irish wolf met its end almost a century later and was probably killed in Co. Carlow, near Mount Leinster, when it was hunted down for killing sheep in 1786.

St Patrick himself was said to have banished all the snakes from Ireland but reptiles, in truth, would not be ideally suited to the Irish climate and had not established themselves in Ireland before the island separated from the landmass of Pangea. One reptile, however, the common lizard, is native to Ireland and can occasionally be spotted in the countryside hiding in dry stone walls, or under rocks or logs during the summer months. There are some amphibians also – you may be fortunate enough to encounter the common frog, natterjack toad or smooth newt in Ireland.

---

24 Hardiman, J., *The History of the Town and County of the Town of Galway* (1820), p.102.

Irish Sea Life

Off the coast, Ireland also has a rich sea life. Turtles are not necessarily native to the seas around Ireland but migratory visitors are often carried here by the prevailing current. The enormous leatherback turtles are the most common visitors and a source of wonder to those who happen to spot them. Conger eels, which have been known to grow up to 3m long, can also be spotted in Irish waters, and in times past may even have been mistaken for sea monsters.

Dolphins are common off the west coast of Ireland. This much-loved creature is the subject of fascination, with many dolphin-watching trips available. The most common species in Irish waters are the short-beaked common dolphin and the bottlenose dolphin. Fungie was undoubtedly the most famous of the species in Ireland. He was an exceptionally friendly bottlenose dolphin who lived around Dingle Harbour in Co. Kerry. Eager to interact with humans, he was an enormous tourist attraction from his first sighting in 1983. In 2020, he was seen for the last time and the local community eventually came to the realisation that he would not be coming back. A statue to the beloved dolphin has now been erected in the town. Blue whales have also been spotted off the Irish coast on very rare occasions in the late summer, although killer and humpback whales are far more common visitors.

Basking sharks are common in Irish waters. Known in Irish as ainmhí sheoil, the beast with the sail, they can grow up to 12m long, making them the second largest sharks in the world, although they are not dangerous to humans. They are in fact slow to flee from human contact and at one time they were hunted by spear-wielding Irish fishermen, mainly for the oil in their liver, which could be used to power lamps or sold on to make other products. Seals were another animal to be hunted occasionally, as the famous 1888 Irish painting 'The Seal Diver' by W.H. Bartlett attests. Ireland has two types of seals: the common and the larger grey. These animals also had an important place in Irish mythology and selkies, or 'seal folk', were believed to be seals that could shed their skins to become human. It was believed that they normally lived in the sea but occasionally transformed into humans and came to land. In the west of Ireland, the surname Conneely was synonymous with selkies and occasionally they were known as the seal people. Strange but true.

Afterword

There are thousands of other remarkable things about Ireland, far too many to mention in this book. It is a very diverse country in terms of its geography. The island is said to be shaped like a teddy bear, with its hair in Antrim and the arms outstretching from Galway. It is mountainous in tracts of the west, with other large mountain ranges in the east, such as the Mournes in Co. Down and the Wicklow Mountains. The central lowlands lie in the middle with the largest peat bog in the world, the Bog of Allen, in their midst. Unsurprisingly, millions of tourists visit Ireland each year. Many travel to the capital, while others visit the Wild Atlantic Way, the longest coastal driving route in the world. Ireland's Ancient East is another tourist route that meanders through Ireland's hidden heartlands, and is increasingly popular with visitors looking to get off the beaten track. The country also boasts a longer river than can be found anywhere in the neighbouring United Kingdom, in the form of the Shannon. Lough Neagh, measuring 19 miles by 9 miles, is also larger than any lake on our neighbouring island. Carrauntoohil, at over 3,400ft, is the largest mountain in Ireland, while Dublin's Phoenix Park is the biggest park in any urban centre in Europe.

Ireland boasts festivals such as the Puck Fair in Killorglin, Co. Kerry, where each August a wild goat is captured in the nearby MacGillycuddy Reeks Mountains and crowned king of the town, a tradition that can be definitively traced back to the 1600s but may even have pre-Christian origins. There is a national leprechaun hunt in Co. Louth, Tedfest on the Aran Islands celebrating the brilliant Irish sitcom *Father Ted*, an annual Red-Haired Convention,

Charlie Chaplin.

a bog-snorkelling championship and a ploughing championship that attracts up to 300,000 visitors each year. Unsurprisingly, many luminaries are fascinated by Ireland. John Lennon of the Beatles purchased his own island in Clew Bay off Co. Mayo. The English actor Jeremy Irons bought and restored a fifteenth-century castle in Co. Cork. Even Charlie Chaplin, whose great-grandmother was from Ireland, visited Co. Kerry regularly on holiday, and a statue of the actor and avid fisherman can be visited in the town of Waterville in the county today.

Ireland contains Sean's Bar, a pub in Athlone, Co. Westmeath, which dates from AD 900 and is one of the oldest hostelries in the world, and a hotel at Woodenbridge, in Wicklow, open since 1608 and still going strong. There is Hook Head Lighthouse, one of the oldest operational lighthouses in the world. There are the Croaghaun Cliffs on Achill Island, the second-highest sea cliffs in Europe, towering nearly 700m above the Atlantic Ocean. There is the Guinness Storehouse, Ireland's most visited tourist attraction, where a pint of the black stuff is at its best. We also have the world's largest amateur sports stadium, Croke Park, which packs in over 82,000 spectators. And much, much more. Ireland always was a truly strange and wonderful place and it remains so to this day.

Select Bibliography

Primary Sources

Census General Reports
Central Statistics Office Reports
Dáil Debates
Down Survey, 1658
Folklore Commission (Schools' Collection), 1937
Griffith's General Valuation of Rateable Property in Ireland, 1855
Newspapers: *Freeman's Journal*, *Irish Times*, *Irish Independent*, *Connaught Telegraph*, *Irish Examiner*, *Belfast Telegraph*, *The Nation*, etc.
RTE Archives

Contemporary Publications and Secondary Sources

Barry, T., *Guerilla Days in Ireland* (Dublin: Irish Press, 1949).

Cambrensis, G., *The History and Topography of Ireland* (translated from the Latin by John J. O'Meara) (New York: Penguin, 1982).

Connolly, J., *Labour in Irish History. The Re-Conquest of Ireland* (Dublin: Maunsel and Roberts, 1910).

Cooney, J., *John Charles McQuaid; Ruler of Catholic Ireland* (Syracuse: Syracuse University Press, 1999).

Da Latocnaye, C., *A Frenchman's Walk through Ireland* (Belfast: McCaw, 1797).

Davitt, M., Carla Kings (eds.), *Jottings in Solitary* (Dublin: UCD Press, 2003).

Dirrane, B., *A Woman of Aran* (Dublin: Blackwater, 2003).

Guiney, L., *Robert Emmet* (London: David Nutt, 1904).

Hardiman, J., *The History of the Town and the County of the Town of Galway from the earliest Period to the Present Time* (Dublin: Folds, 1820).

Jackson, A., *The Origins, Politics and Culture of Irish Unionism, 1880–1916* (Cambridge: Cambridge University Press, 2018).

Joycelyn, R., *Progress of the Reformation in Ireland* (London: James Nisbet, 1851).

Kavanagh, J., *The Irish Assassins: Conspiracy, Revenge and the Murder that Stunned an Empire* (Glasgow: Grove Press, 2021).

Kearns, K., *Dublin's Lost Heroines; Mammies and Grannies in a Vanished City* (Dublin: Gill, 2006).

Lewis, S., *A Topographical Directory of Ireland* (London: S. Lewis Collection, 1837).

McAnally, D.R., *Irish Wonders* (New York: Weathervane, 1888).

Mac Gregor, G., *The History of Burke and Hare* (Glasgow: Morison, 1884).

McNally, M., *Ireland 1649–52: Cromwell's Protestant Crusade* (Oxford: Osprey Publishing, 2009).

Mansfield, M.F & B.M., *Romantic Ireland* (Boston: Page & Co., 1904).

Munck, R. & Rolston, B., *Belfast in the 1930s; An Oral History* (New York: St Martin's, 1997).

Nicholson, A., *Ireland's Welcome to the Stranger* (New York: Baker and Scribner, 1847).

O'Rourke, J., *History of the Irish Famine* (Chicago: University of Illinois, 1902).

Prichard, J., *An Account of the Ladies of Llangollen* (Llangollen: Jones, 1923).
Robinson, P., *Understanding Northern Ireland – A Part of the United Kingdom* (Belfast: Democratic Unionist Party, 1996).
Spenser, E., *A View of the Present State of Ireland* (Oxford: Clarendon, 1970).
Sullivan, A.M., *The Story of Ireland; a Narrative of Irish History, from the earliest Ages to the Insurrection of 1867* (Providence: McElroy, 1883).
Synge, J.M., *Travels in Wicklow, West Kerry and Connemara* (Dublin: Maunsel & Co., 1911).
Wilde, J., *Ancient Legends, Mystic Charms & Superstitions of Ireland* (Boston: Ticknor, 1888).
Woodham-Smith, C., *The Great Hunger: The Story of the Potato Famine of the 1840s* (Alexandria: Oldtown Books, 1962).
Yeats, W.B., *Irish Fairy Tales* (London: Walter Scott, 1890).